Wineries of the Great Lakes:
A Guidebook

Designed by Marilyn Appleby Design
Edited by Ruth A. Moen
Library of Congress Catalog Card Number 95-69354
ISBN 1-881892-03-4
Printed and bound in the United States of America

Published by Spradlin & Associates,
P.O. Box 863, Lapeer, MI 48446. Telephone (810) 664-8406.
First Edition.

Although the author and publisher have exhaustively
researched all sources to ensure the accuracy and completeness of
the information contained in this book, we assume no responsibility
for error, inaccuracies, omissions or any inconsistency herein.
Any slights of people or organizations are unintentional.

Cover photo courtesy of The Michigan Grape
and Wine Industry Council.

RAPTOR PRESS

Raptor Press is an imprint of Spradlin & Associates

Wineries of the
Great Lakes

A Guidebook

1ST EDITION

JOE BORRELLO

Preface
& Acknowledgments

WINERIES OF THE GREAT LAKES: A GUIDEBOOK is a compilation of 133 wineries that make up the unique winegrowing regions experiencing the beneficial influence of "lake effect" weather conditions. Though there are more wineries in the states addressed by this book, only those wineries whose growing conditions are directly affected by the Great Lakes have been included. Consequently, Northwestern Indiana, the Lake Erie regions of New York, Ohio and Pennsylvania, all of Michigan and Ontario, the Finger Lakes region of New York and the Door Peninsula of Wisconsin are the subject of this endeavor.

It should be noted that the eastern winery industry is in the midst of an aggressive growth pattern and some of the wineries in this book will likely change hands, names and indeed, new wineries will appear on the scene after publication. To get an up-to-date list of wineries, contact specific state or provincial wine associations. Since some of the small farm wineries are seasonal, a phone call will give up-to-date visiting and touring hours of the facilities.

It would not have been possible to complete this book without the publications and invaluable assistance from the staffs of:

The Indiana Wine Grape Council
The Michigan Grape and Wine Industry Council
The New York Wine & Grape Foundation
The Ohio Wine Producers Association
The Wine Council of Ontario

The author is also indebted to Leon D. Adams, author of *The Wines of America*, for his guidance through the eastern wine regions; to Ruth Moen, who as copy editor of this book assured minimal damage to the English language and to Barbara Borrello, for without her patience, encouragement and wifely persistence, this book may never have been completed.

DEDICATION

To the many members of the family farm wineries
of the Great Lakes who have
dedicated themselves to the perpetuation
of our pleasure through wine.

Contents

Introduction

From Wisconsin's Door Peninsula to New York's Finger Lakes, winery personnel constantly receive inquiries from visitors to their Great Lakes tasting rooms for a wine to compare with a particular European variety. Quite frequently, after sampling a suggested wine, the guest experiences a surprisingly new, yet familiar, taste sensation.

Distinct characteristics in flavor and bouquet are found in the wines of the Great Lakes even though much of its grape growing regions are on the same land parallels as some of the famous European wine districts. The differences are due to the unique soils of the area created by glacier movement during the Ice Age. These same glaciers also carved out enormous bodies of water in the middle of a huge land mass. These large, deep lakes (all the Great Lakes and the Finger Lakes) have a marked affect on the weather conditions of the land adjoining them to the east and southeast. The warmth of the lakes from the summer sun is retained well into fall and tempers the cool air coming in from the west and northwest. This allows for a longer growing season, sometimes into mid or late November. In the spring, the cold water cools off the warm breezes so the vines do not bud too soon and become exposed to a sudden spring frost. The combination of weather patterns and the topography of the glacial-scarred land creates micro-climates or pockets of discernible temperate weather zones that directly affect the growth of agricultural crops.

It is this micro-climate phenomenon that accounts for the creation of the magnificent Icewines of Ontario, the luscious Late Harvest wines of Michigan's Leelanau and Old Mission Peninsulas and the extraordinary Rieslings of New York's Finger Lakes and...viticulturists are just beginning to learn how to best utilize these micro-climates and distinctive soils. European winemakers have had centuries to learn how to adapt to nature. Great Lakes growers have only been at it for a few decades, but the results have been notable! From the "juice grapes" of the native American varieties such as Concord and Niagara, wineries have progressed to the hearty and bountiful French-American hybrids like Seyval, Vidal, Vignoles and Chancellor. More recently (within the last decade), we have seen a remarkable proficiency in the development of classic European grape varieties such as Riesling, Chardonnay, Pinot Noir and Cabernet Franc.

The achievements of Great Lakes wineries in quality and know-how are compounding rapidly. In the mid-1980's, noted American wine author, Leon D. Adams, commented to me, "The quality of Midwest and Eastern wines has increased so much, it borders on being dramatic." A decade later, it is *definitely* dramatic. Along with the enormous strides in agricultural development, each new vintage demonstrates consistent advancement in winemaking technique, technology and competence in the critical area of vineyard management.

Almost every winemaker will tell you, "great wines are made in the vineyard." Those same winemakers may also say, "You can make bad wine from good grapes, but you can't make good wine from bad grapes." As the different wine areas note their progress and realize their potential, they'll strive for the ultimate in quality and begin to pledge to the consumer the very best of their efforts. Associations such as Ontario's Vintners Quality Alliance (VQA) and the Lake Erie Quality Wine Alliance are the first coalitions that have been founded to educate and assure the consumer of quality products. More are sure to follow.

The topic of wine is fascinating and often times emotional. It is a simple agricultural product, yet many have a tendency to shroud it in mystery and complexity. It is important to realize that wine has been placed on dining tables for centuries as a natural beverage that serves as a pleasing and logical companion to food.

Few other products offer as much diverse subject matter as wine. Interests range from cultivating personal vineyards, visiting the actual property of a winery, collecting wine labels, building a wine collection of fine wines, to simply taste-testing different wine styles with friends.

Wine also combines instinctively with an interest in food. Many professional and amateur chefs are wine hobbyists because good cuisine demands wine both as an intricate seasoning ingredient and as a basic component of the dining table. Keep in mind that like food, it is important to create a point of reference for what you may like in wine. As time goes by and your tasting experience grows you will notice subtle differences in your preferences. It is helpful to seek information from others, but don't be intimidated by their opinions.

Although many hours could be spent studying the finer points of wine makeup, it is best enjoyed as an uncomplicated subject. So, what is the best way to enjoy and learn about wine and food? The experts tell us there is no substitute for personal tasting experiences. Through taste comes the acquisition of knowledge. What better way to acquire knowledge than by visiting Great Lakes wineries or gathering with a group of friends for a wine and food tasting? As you taste and compare wines you will find that not all are pleasing to you, and that's how it should be. Wine, like food, is made in many different styles to satisfy different tastes. It is up to the individual to choose the wines that best suit a personal palate and pocketbook. In the Great Lakes region we are fortunate to have over 150 winery tasting room facilities in which to experience a variety of tastes and styles of wine. Many of the wineries have educational tours and videos of the facilities and the winemaking process. Knowledgeable winery representatives then guide visitors through enchanting tasting tours of nature's fruit of the vine.

Experience the treasures and the pleasures of wine for yourself, follow the designated signs of the "wine trails and routes" through any of the Great Lakes' alluring winemaking areas. Hopefully, this book will be a useful guide in your adventure.

"Moderation is essential to the enjoyment of everything."

—Ralph Waldo Emerson

Lake Superior

Lake Huron

Old Mission Peninsula

Traverse City

Green Bay

Wisconsin

Michigan

Lake Michigan

Grand Rapids

Detroit

Windsor

Milwaukee

Paw Paw

Chicago

Toledo

Illinois

Gary

Indiana

Ohio

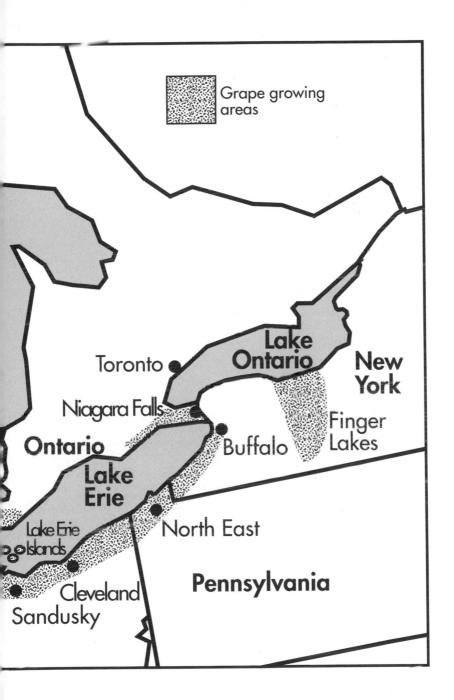

Grape growing areas

Toronto

Niagara Falls

Lake Ontario

New York

Ontario

Finger Lakes

Buffalo

Lake Erie

Lake Erie Islands

North East

Cleveland

Sandusky

Pennsylvania

INDIANA

The nation's first successful commercial vineyard was established in 1802 by several families of Swiss vine-dressers (those who tend or care for grapevines) in the southeastern part of Indiana. Later, other immigrants from France and Germany also settled in the state and pursued viticultural activity. The early Indiana grape and wine industry survived disease and severe weather to become at one point, the 10th largest grape-producing state in the U.S. But, like so many others, fifteen years of Prohibition destroyed the hard work and dreams of the country's grape farming pioneers.

The Hoosier state is not particularly noted in industry circles for its current wine production, but it's moving ahead thanks to the efforts of some adventurous dreamers and the assistance of Purdue University. In 1989, the Indiana General Assembly contributed to the cause by establishing the Indiana Wine Grape Council to "enhance economic development by developing a successful wine grape industry through research and marketing." This action was a follow-up to the state's passage of the Small Winery Law in 1971 which allowed wineries to sell directly to the public. Today, visitors to the wineries can sample a wide range of wines from dry to sweet that are made from French/American hybrids, *vinifera* and native American grape varieties as well as Indiana fruit. Nearly ninety percent of Indiana wines are sold out of winery tasting rooms. At this point, tourism is the key to the success of the wine industry and the Council's focal point of marketing.

Of the thirteen wineries in Indiana, only two are located in the Northern section of the state which would be affected by the Great Lakes climate. Lake Michigan Winery buys most of its grapes from vineyards in the Evanston area and from growers just across the state border in the bountiful Southwestern Michigan grape region. Anderson's Orchard & Winery relies on its production of fruit wines based primarily on its abundant supply of apples. Both operations are a long way from stardom, but they have high hopes, ambition, energy and enthusiasm - key elements to any successful venture and a reflection of the influence of early settlers.

Even as we approach the turn of a new century and an era of high technology, the tenacity of the North American farmer to work the land in harmony with nature is never more evident than it is in Indiana and across the Great Lakes region.

For more information on Indiana's grape and wine industry, contact:
The Indiana Wine Grape Council, Building 20, Ste 2004,
5610 Crawfordsville Road, Indianapolis, IN 46224
(317) 481-0222 or 1-800-832-WINE

Anderson's Orchard & Winery

LOCATION: 430 East U.S. Highway 6
                    Valparaiso, IN 46383
                    (219) 464-4936

HOURS: 9 AM to 6 PM, Mon.-Sat.
                    11 AM to 5 PM, Sunday

AMENITIES: Country Market, Wine tastings,
                    Cross-country ski trails

The Anderson family's orchard began in 1927 as a small roadside market next to a beautiful 40-acre parcel of land in Porter County. In 1954, Bill Anderson expanded the family business to over five thousand fruit-filled trees containing over 15 different varieties of "some of the best eatin' apples you've ever had", according to David Lundstrom, the current owner of Anderson's Orchard and Winery.

Lundstrom added the winery in the fall of '94 after he purchased the property from the retiring Bill Anderson. "Bill had no family to take over the business and it was always a dream of mine to open a winery," explains Lundstrom, "I just feel it's the most ideal lifestyle a man could have. There's no greater joy than sitting around, drinking wine and watching your grapes grow," he chuckles.

The foundation of the Anderson Winery is the orchard's sizable production of apples. "We sit on a very unique piece of land that is the highest ground in the area and only five miles from Lake Michigan. This gives us a very favorable micro-climate for fruit growing," says Lundstrom. "Even with all the harsh and unpredictable weather that can happen around the southern tip of the lake, we haven't lost an apple crop since we started in 1954."

Lundstrom is making the most out of his good fortune. The Anderson Country Market is filled with apple ciders (sweet and hard), apple-based wines (strawberry/apple, rhubarb/apple, raspberry/apple and more), and a new bakery that specializes in, you guessed it, apple strudel. "I make the best apple strudel you've ever had in your life," he boasts.

Beyond the homemade apple butters, jams and jellies, pastry and wines, Lundstrom also produces a limited amount of grape wines from his small vineyard. Anderson's is also a major supplier of juice and supplies for amateur beer and winemakers, as well. Besides keeping up with all of the above, all Lundstrom has to do is "sit around and watch my grapes grow." Not!

Lake Michigan Winery

LOCATION: US 41
            (Calumet Ave. at 119Th St.)
            Whiting, IN 46394
            (219) 659-3501

HOURS: 1 PM to 7 PM, Daily

AMENITIES: Tasting & retail room
            Tours

WINEMAKERS CHOICE OF THE YEAR

STRAWBERRY

TABLE WINE   CONTAINS SULFITES
THOMAS F. OWENS
816 - 119th Street, Whiting, Indiana. 46394. Ph.219•659•3501
For Sale In Indiana Only

Lake Michigan Winery first planted grapes in 1986 around Madison, in southern Indiana, near the Kentucky border. In 1992, a fire ravaged the 10 acres of French hybrid grape vines. The vineyard was plowed under and owner Tom Owens moved his operation to the north, near one of the largest wine markets in the Midwest - Chicago.

The Lake Michigan Winery was built just six blocks from a new 1200-boat marina on the Indiana shore of Lake Michigan. The building is a unique structure of brick, concrete and steel beams that one may guess would house an art studio. Indeed art is the subject, albeit the art of making wine.

Winemaker Henry Cunningham crafts 15 to 16 wines from grapes and fruit grown by area farmers, including those just across the border in Michigan. The Lake Michigan Winery portfolio includes the French hybrid wines of Vidal, Foch and Chancellor as well as fruit wines of apple, pear, cherry, blueberry and a popular favorite - Lake Michigan Strawberry.

A tour of the winery takes you beneath the building and the typical moldy aroma of a wine cellar where nearly 10,000 gallons of wine are aged in stainless steel and oak vats. At the other end of the cellar is the scrubbed floor and polished stainless steel tanks of the actual working winery where sanitation is a top priority for making good wine.

At the end of the tour visitors are invited to taste the product and look through a variety of wine accessories available in the retail room. The inventory here ranges from numerous wine art items, to exotic corkscrews and, of course, the ever-present T-shirt touting, in this case, "Indiana Wine - A Grape Idea".

Its a fun visit to the Lake Michigan Winery and its easily accessible. If you're in the area, stop by and take in the antiques, stained glass and a free wine tasting. Who knows, you may even take some wine home or send it to a friend.

MICHIGAN

All along the Lake Michigan shoreline of Michigan, from the Indiana border north to Grand Traverse Bay, there is a bounty of luscious fruit. The land and the micro-climates here are well-suited for hearty cool-weather fruit. A number of hybrid and vinifera grape varieties thrive within this environment and vineyards continue to spring up from Paw Paw to the Leelanau and Old Mission peninsulas.

Michigan enjoys a wide spectrum of wine styles due to the varying weather patterns and lengths of the growing season between the southern and northern regions. Add to these conditions, Italian, French, German and California winemaking influences among Michigan's winemakers, and visitors will likely find a taste that will satisfy any individual palate.

The most popular of the state's wine styles is the soft, semi-dry white wines of Vidal Blanc and Riesling. These wines, with their prominent fruit flavor and flowery bouquet, are reminiscent of German products. Because Germany and Michigan have similar cool climate conditions, their grapes have a tendency to evolve to the same desired sugar, fruit acid and alcohol levels that provide for the soft, fruity and extremely palatable wines that appeal to most wine consumers.

Michigan winemakers also strive to accommodate those who favor the traditional French techniques and nuances of winemaking. Seyval, Vignoles and Chardonnay are produced in both the full-bodied, oak version of Burgundy and the crisper stainless steel finish akin to other prestigious French appellations.

The European art of "blending" has become prevalent throughout the state in the last few years. Using the best quality grapes available from a given harvest, Michigan winemakers determined that they can often blend a calculated selection of different grape varieties to produce a better product. Under a multitude of generic names the wines are well-received by inquiring consumers.

Although current customer appeal and production emphasis is centered on the highly successful Michigan white wines, the emergence of red wine is fast becoming noteworthy. Chancellor and Chambourcin are two premium dry red wine grapes establishing a distinguished reputation in Southwest Michigan. By themselves, or preferably blended together, these French hybrid grapes bear many of the same desirable complexities and deep rich color of the better known Cabernet Sauvignon from California and from the Bordeaux region of France. When aged for a few years, partially in wood, Chancellor and Chambourcin based wines are welcome guests at any dinner table.

Some encouraging examples of the world-famous Pinot Noir and Pinot Gris grapes are also beginning to emerge in both the north and south growing regions of the state. As table wines or as integral parts of Michigan's promising premium sparkling wine industry, these European varieties are delicious and exciting experiments in tasting rooms throughout the state.

The continued research and experimentation by growers and winemakers in cooperation with the Horticulture Department of Michigan State University produces impressive results with each new crop. From the southern to the northern regions of the state, a variety of distinctive styles and tastes exist. Wine enthusiasts must experiment in the tasting rooms to note each vintner's signature contribution to the continuing development of Michigan's wine industry.

For more information and brochures on Michigan wineries, contact:
The Michigan Grape and Wine Industry Council
P.O. Box 30017
Lansing, MI 48909
(517) 373-1958

Boskydel Vineyard

LOCATION: Route 1, Box 522
            Lake Leelanau, MI 49653
            (Northwest of Traverse City)
            (616) 256-7272

HOURS: Every day 1-6 PM
            Open year round

AMENITIES: Free wine tasting,
            Retail sales

SOLEIL BLANC
LEELANAU PENINSULA TABLE WINE
A DRY, WHITE

PRODUCED AND BOTTLED BY BOSKYDEL
VINEYARD, LAKE LEELANAU, MI, BWC-MI-42

It is common among winemakers to be independent, strong-willed and somewhat unconventional. Although Bernie Rink of Boskydel Vineyards may fit this characteristic profile, he will be remembered by future generations primarily for his contribution of introducing grape-growing and winemaking in Northern Michigan.

Since 1964 Rink has experimented with over 35 varieties of wine grapes in vineyards near a grove of pines overlooking Lake Leelanau, just north of Traverse City. Boskydel's twenty-five acres of vineyards thrive on a sunny slope that is oriented to the southwest — a site that affords the grapes enough warmth and sunlight to reach the maturity needed to produce table wines at this latitude. The grapes are French-American hybrids that combine the wine quality of French vines with the disease-resistance of American roots. The wines derived from these marriages are definitely European in character and range from good to excellent. Each varietal and blend is distinctive in bouquet and body - fruity when young and mellow when aged. As visitors will discover, Boskydel varietals such as Vignoles, Soleil Blanc and De Chaunac have a magic all their own. Boskydel Red, White and Rosé blends will approximate and often exceed good *vin ordinaires* from France.

Beyond his numerous vineyard plantings, Rink has planted Christmas trees and chestnut trees. This latest venture moved Suzanne Rink to jokingly write her husband's epitaph, "He ran out of things to plant, so he planted himself."   Bernie Rink is also fond of philosophizing, it's an outgrowth of his numerous years as the librarian for Northwestern Michigan College in Traverse City. Nearly any day of the year will find from one to any number of people in the tasting room just "shooting the breeze" or solving the problems of the world while listening to classical music and enjoying a well-made glass of Boskydel wine.

Bowers Harbor Vineyards

LOCATION: 2896 Bowers Harbor Road
Old Mission Peninsula
Traverse City, MI 49684
(616) 223-7615

HOURS: Mon.- Sat. 11-6 PM
Sun. 12-6 PM, Year round

AMENITIES: Free wine tasting,
Retail sales and gift shop

Jack Stegenga opened a stockbroker's office in Traverse City, Michigan in 1969 and since that time has extended himself to additional careers as a restaurateur and rancher. In the 80's his restaurant interest led him to the wine country of Germany where a new passion began to take seed. Jack and his wife Linda, continued to visit other wine-growing regions in Italy, France and Australia. With each visit the couple learned more about growing grapes and making wine.

In 1990, Stegenga entered into an agreement with a winemaker neighbor to produce and market wine under the newly formed Bowers Harbor Vineyards label. The farm/ranch of the Stegenga's was transformed into five acres of vineyards featuring premium Chardonnay and Riesling grapes. Within a short time Bowers Harbor Vineyards gained recognition and popularity by earning competitive awards for their wines.

"In just a few years our production has reached over 2,000 cases and our goal is 5,000, but that's it," claims Stegenga, "We would like to see new wineries on the peninsula develop, but we'll remain a small boutique premium winery, that way we will all enjoy the fruits of our wonderful area." Stegenga's optimism for the area is well-founded since the natural rolling hills of the Old Mission Peninsula lie on the same forty-fifth parallel as the renowned vineyards of Europe.   And like Europe, the vineyards are also protected by a body of water that tempers the climate.

Bowers Harbor has a charming tasting room at the vineyard site just off M-37 on the peninsula. It is a beautiful drive with stunning bay views and picturesque rolling acreage of orchards and thriving vinifera grapes. Linda Stegenga oversees the day-to-day retail operation at Bowers Harbor where visitors can sample and buy premium Chardonnay, Riesling, sparkling wine and wine-related gifts. As the Stegenga's so accurately express, "A wine-tasting trip to Bowers Harbor Vineyards is a gift to the senses."

Chateau Chantal

LOCATION: 15900 Rue de Vin
Old Mission Peninsula
Traverse City, MI 49684
(616) 223-4110

HOURS: Mon.-Sat. 11-5,
Sun. 12-5, Year round

AMENITIES: Free wine tasting, Retail sales,
Guided tours, Bed & Breakfast rooms,
Private party facilities

1991
Chardonnay
Old Mission Peninsula
Alcohol 11.6% by Vol.

The picturesque landscape settings of the Old Mission peninsula are personified at the majestic estate of Chateau Chantal, which features northern Michigan's only bed and breakfast winery. Popular Michigan winemaker Mark Johnson joins grape-grower Bob Begin in this ambitious venture of creating an "Old World" atmosphere within a magnificent and stately structure that offers some of the most spectacular winery scenery in the Great Lakes. The winery site straddles a ridge near the northern end of the peninsula about twelve miles north of Traverse City. Nearly every part of the property offers stunning views of either side of Lake Michigan's Grand Traverse Bay, which is split by the narrow 20 mile long strip of fertile land.

The area has long been a coveted secret as a favorite summer and winter vacation spot. The peninsula's primary agricultural industry is cherry and grape-growing. Chateau Chantal has been designed not only to physically fit within the scenic environment, but also to offer a quality product line and lodging that are in keeping with the area's growing reputation for fine foods, exceptional hospitality and superb wines.

The primary grape varieties grown at Chateau Chantal are Chardonnay, Riesling, Gewurztraminer and Pinot Blanc for white wines and Pinot Noir and Merlot for the reds. Johnson and Begin also have smaller plantings of Cabernet Franc, Pinot Meunier and Nebbiolo which are being carefully evaluated for their commercial potential.

The romance and wonders of nature are intricate parts of the philosophy of Chateau Chantal and the presentation of their wine. From the vineyard, to the winery, to the tasting room, a feeling of man being one with nature is strongly evident in this most breathtaking of settings. With Chantal's private "bed & breakfast" suites overlooking the hillside vineyards and the unequaled ambiance of Chateau's "Great Room", one will easily escape the pressures of daily life and be engulfed in the serenity of a personal retreat.

Chateau Grand Traverse

LOCATION: 12239 Center Road
Old Mission Peninsula
Traverse City, MI 49686
(616) 223-7355

HOURS: Mon.- Sat. 10-5 PM
Sun. Noon-5 PM
Year round

AMENITIES: Free wine tasting, Retail sales,
Cellar tour in summer season,
Cellarmaster's Club

What would motivate a successful businessman to risk his assets and venture into the precarious world of making wine in an area that all the "experts" said was too unpredictable? Edward O'Keefe quips, "Back in 1974, people must have thought I had more money than brains. They said the Northern Michigan climate could only be withstood by American hybrid grapes. I wanted to grow European Vinifera grapes and my research indicated that it could be done. I wanted to prove that world-class wine could be made in Michigan."

Armed with carefully calculated research, consultations with expert European viticulturists and the tenacity of his Irish heritage, O'Keefe pursued his vision of a "world-class" winery on the Old Mission Peninsula north of Traverse City. As Ed O'Keefe, Jr. is fond of saying, "Chateau Grand Traverse was my father's 'Field of Dreams' - just build it and they will come!"

Choosing the winery location on the highest point of the peninsula was relatively easy, the difficult part was moving more than one million cubic yards of earth to achieve a complete southwest exposure to the sun. This allows the vines to maximize the growing season necessary for premium European grape varieties.

From that early commitment to plant primarily Riesling and Chardonnay grapes, Chateau Grand Traverse continued to experiment with other varieties. As O'Keefe recounts, "Although I knew in my soul we could make white wines, I wasn't so sure Michigan was the place to make good red wines." Today, the O'Keefe's are happy about their red wine production of Pinot Noir and Merlot and are particularly enthusiastic about the development of Gamay, a crisp, fruity red wine that in the last few years has become a tasting room favorite.

The O'Keefes are committed to their original mission of producing fine Vinifera wines and are still setting new goals in establishing Chateau Grand Traverse as "Michigan's World-Class Winery."

Fenn Valley Vineyards and Winery

LOCATION: 6130 122nd Ave.
            Fennville, MI 49408
            (I-96 to Exit 34, follow the signs)
            (800) 432-6265

HOURS: Mon.- Sat. 10-5,
            Sun. 1-5, Year round

AMENITIES: Free wine tasting, Retail sales,
            Self-guided tour, Picnic area and
            patio with grill, Private party facilities,
            Special food demonstration promotions

A love for family winemaking and an extensive research program brought the William Welsch family in 1973 to the little farm and orchard community of Fennville in southwest Michigan. Equipped with a degree in chemistry, the financial security of a successful building-supply company and a winemaking son with a biology background, Welsch took on the odds against success in the wine business.

Winemaker Doug Welsch has nurtured, through a continuous series of experiments, the premium hybrid wine grapes of Chancellor, Seyval, Vidal and Vignoles which are well-suited for Michigan weather and soil. He has also cultivated thriving plantings of the Riesling, Gewurztraminer, Pinot Gris, Pinot Noir and Chardonnay vinifera grapes of Europe.

Fenn Valley Winery has distinguished itself with many national medals and awards, but most recently the winery has also been identified as being on the cutting edge of a new concept in the wine industry. The Michigan winery is one of only a handful of wineries in the country producing "de-alcoholized" wines. Since this product is first vinified as a wine, then the alcohol is removed, it offers taste sensations that are more appropriate with food consumption than the sweeter "non-alcoholic" grape-juice drinks commonly offered in grocery stores.

Welsch's reverse osmosis process for making de-alcoholized wine is so complete that the finished product is measured to have less natural fruit alcohol than commercial orange juice. Using premium grape varieties such as Chardonnay, Cabernet Sauvignon and Sauvignon Blanc, Fenn Valley has developed a complete line of de-alcoholized wines for every taste including a popular sparkling champagne-style product.

Good Harbor Vineyards

GOOD HARBOR®

1991 Fishtown White
Michigan

Dry White Table Wine, Produced and Bottled By
Good Harbor Vineyards, Lake Leelanau, MI 49653   BW-MI-49
Net Contents 50.7 fl. oz. (1500 ml)

LOCATION:	Leland, MI 49653
	(M-22 three miles south of Leland)
	(616) 256-7165
HOURS:	Mon.- Sat. 11-5 PM
	Sun. Noon-5 PM, May 20-Nov.1
AMENITIES:	Free wine tasting, Retail sales,
	Self-guided tour, Farm market

Bruce Simpson is not the high-profile sort of winemaker seen making the speaking circuit these days. Simpson prefers to allow his popular Good Harbor wines to speak for themselves.

With his experience in the family's orchard business, Simpson felt confident that Michigan, and in particular the Leelanau Peninsula, was more than adequately capable of producing quality grapes to make award-winning wine. It was just a matter of selecting the right wine-grape varieties for the area's soil and climatic conditions, which he admits treads on the edge of efficient viticulture.

Since the introduction of wine grapes at Good Harbor in 1978, experimentation and research have prompted the soft-spoken winemaker to concentrate on the grape varieties of Johannisberg Riesling, Seyval, Vignoles, Pinot Gris and some Chardonnay.

The Johannisberg Riesling and Chardonnay wines of Good Harbor are highly regarded for their mouth-filling fruit flavor and wonderfully balanced acidity that resemble their European counterparts more than their California cousins. Simpson is also excited about his Pinot Gris, a member of the grape family that includes Pinot Noir and Pinot Blanc. This delicate wine is a lovely companion for most seafood and shellfish. A best-seller is "Fishtown White", named after the historic Fishtown area of nearby Leland. This fairly dry white wine is a blend of Seyval and Vignoles and is the perfect dinner companion for any fish or seafood entree.

Though Simpson professes to be a pure farmer and winemaker, he is generally credited for introducing one of Michigan's most successful marketing coups with the introduction of the best-selling "Trillium". This semi-dry, white wine blend of Seyval, Vignoles, Vidal and Riesling, with its colorful rendition of the Trillium flower on the label, brought instant recognition to retail shelves and overnight success for the winery.

The labels of Good Harbor also display vivid graphics of the scenic Leelanau countryside, but more importantly Good Harbor wines fulfill the pursuit of an unassuming winemaker who desires only to grow and produce the finest wine possible and offer good consumer value.

Heart of the Vineyard Winery

LOCATION: 10981 Hills Road
            (Exit 16 off I-94)
            Baroda, MI 49101
            (616) 422-1617

HOURS: Daily Noon to 6 PM
            Memorial Day to Labor Day
            Fri., Sat., Sun. & Mon. after
            Labor Day

AMENITIES: Wine tastings & tours, Retail sales,
            Bed & Breakfast facility,
            Special wine theme events

The Heart of the Vineyard Winery, with its tasting room and gift shop, is housed in an 1881 post and beam bank barn. You can sample wines inside the hand-hewn barn, or choose to sip your wine on the open-air veranda. Both overlook rolling hills of carefully groomed grape vines.

Winemaker/owner Rick Moersch enlisted the help of some of his European friends to choose and plant a variety of unique grape varieties in his vineyards. These vines include such "old world" names as Gewürztraminer, Scheurebe, Müeller-Thurgau and Riesling, as well as today's "in vogue" varieties like Chardonnay and Pinot Noir. All told, Heart of the Vineyard offers more than 20 varieties of red, white, blush and some notable sparkling wines. Visitors may tour the earth-cooled wine cellar and working champagne cave.

Moersch has a close kinship with Southwestern Michigan wineries starting in 1979 as the winemaker for Tabor Hill Vineyards while he gradually built up his vineyards. In 1992, he struck out on his own and eventually entered into a working agreement with Fenn Valley Vineyards as a sparkling wine consultant to the winery in exchange for production facility services. Today, the accord has benefited both parties and they are looking toward expansion of the partnership.

Moersch, with wife Sherrie, has also created a "country getaway" Bed & Breakfast adjacent to the main house. A spacious room overlooks the vineyard complete with private deck and bath. Guests soak up the rural country setting with long walks or a session in the outdoor hot tub. Private wine tasting and extra wine discounts are included. However, the Heart of the Vineyard Bed & Breakfast is booked well in advance, so a well-planned phone call for reservations is necessary.

As the Moersch's are fond of saying, "Whatever your pleasure...relax, rest, and unwind at Heart of the Vineyard."

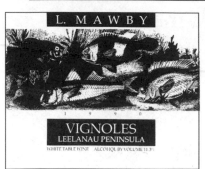

L. Mawby Vineyards

LOCATION: 4519 South Elm Valley Road
Suttons Bay, MI 49682
(616) 271-3522

HOURS: Mon.- Sat. 11-5 PM. Sun. Noon-5 PM
May 20-Nov.1

AMENITIES: Free wine tasting, Retail sales,
Local arts & crafts

*Wine, The Heart of Agriculture / Now in the light fluid colors dance /
as aromas of heaven from earth ascend/& our tongue lies wrapped in / mystery and joy. /
and so we drink the heart of agriculture / & so it is we / are sustained.*

This is the poetry of a pensive and dedicated agriculturist and yet, L. Mawby's finely crafted wines bear such names as "Turkey Red", "P.G.W. Pun" (an actual pun on "Pretty Good Wine"), "Shard O'Neight" and something called "Tattoo". To say that winemaker/owner Larry Mawby is a complex man of humor and intelligence is an understatement. More importantly, he is a man of the earth, a farmer, a lifestyle that fits him more perfectly than an intrusive urban society could offer.

L. Mawby is a small winery producing estate-grown table and *methode champenoise* (bottle-fermented) sparkling wines from twelve acres of vineyards on the hills near Suttons Bay on Michigan's Leelanau Peninsula.

The wines of Mawby are primarily Burgundian in style, dry, full-bodied and barrel-fermented. The climatic conditions of the area are very conducive to this French style with temperatures slightly cooler than Burgundy, France, but also a bit warmer than that of the Champagne region. Mawby has wisely positioned himself to take advantage of fluctuations in the Michigan weather to plan his production between table wines and sparkling wines depending on the year's crop. "We are able to make the very best wine possible, regardless of the weather, by switching our production between sparkling and still wines according to the dictates of a cool or hot growing season," states Mawby.

Since 1984, Mawby has been experimenting with *methode champenoise* sparkling wines much to the enjoyment of "bubbly" enthusiasts. A very different style of sparkling wine offered by the winery is called Cremant. Historically in France, Cremant is considered a style of sparkling wine used for dinner, that has a lower level of effervescence with a creamy texture in the mouth rather than an explosion of effervescence.

Le Montueux Vineyard & Winery

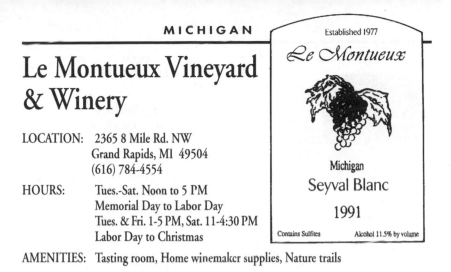

Established 1977

Le Montueux

Michigan

Seyval Blanc

1991

Contains Sulfites   Alcohol 11.5% by volume

LOCATION: 2365 8 Mile Rd. NW
Grand Rapids, MI 49504
(616) 784-4554

HOURS: Tues.-Sat. Noon to 5 PM
Memorial Day to Labor Day
Tues. & Fri. 1-5 PM, Sat. 11-4:30 PM
Labor Day to Christmas

AMENITIES: Tasting room, Home winemaker supplies, Nature trails

LeMontueux Vineyard & Winery (translated as the "hilly vineyard") was founded in 1990. It is a small family-owned operation which actually began in 1977 when the first grape plantings were made. The site is nestled amid rolling terrain carved by glacial action and located 25 miles east of Lake Michigan and ten miles northwest of downtown Grand Rapids. The region is well-known as "The Ridge" which is an area of productive tree fruit in the state.

Owners Rodger and Kathy Woltjer are actively involved in every phase of the winery's production process. Their 55 acre parcel of land is perfectly situated for a vineyard. It has a south slope, high elevation, good drainage and great air circulation, all the necessary components for outstanding grape production. There is plenty of room for expansion and the Woltjer's continue to plant new vines each year between pruning, picking and pressing grapes, bottling and labeling the wine and running the tasting room. The Woltjers are also school teachers who have learned the winemaking process from books by trial and error. Their lessons have been very informative and they have received above-average grades for their achievements.

LeMontueux grows and makes grape wine only from French-American hybrids which are crosses between native American and European grape varieties. The wines are produced only by individual grape variety and are not blended, contrary to current winemaking trends. Rodger Woltjer is dedicated to the philosophy of promoting and educating the consumer on the quality potential of Michigan wines made from hybrids and has sought to elevate their reputation.

LeMontueux also features a small amount of tree fruit wines, local cheese, sausage and bread, home winemaking supplies and the recent addition of nature trails around the winery property. Visitors to the Grand Rapids area, the second largest city in the state, can now add a winery to their list of "sights to see."

LEELANAU CELLARS

RENAISSANCE

Premium Dry White Table Wine
PRODUCED AND BOTTLED BY LEELANAU WINE CELLARS, LTD., OMENA, MICHIGAN 49674

Leelanau Wine Cellars

LOCATION: County Road 626
Omena, MI 49674
(616) 386-5201

HOURS: Mon.- Sat. 11-5 PM
Sun. Noon-5 PM
Year round

AMENITIES: Free wine tasting,
Retail sales

The fastest-growing winemaking area in Michigan seems to be in the northwest region of the state. Contributing to this accelerated growth is the area's largest winery - Leelanau Wine Cellars, located in Omena just north of Suttons Bay on the Leelanau Peninsula.

In recent years the winery has achieved national honors for its highly successful "Tall Ships" Chardonnay, a wine that consistently sells out each vintage. Another marketing accomplishment was the creation of the popular "Vis-a-Vis" wines. The white version is half Chardonnay and half Vignoles. The red wine counterpart is a blend of Pinot Noir and Baco Noir. Both wines are perfect examples of how the classic Vinifera and the French hybrid grape varieties work well together in the Great Lakes region.

Leelanau also offers a new blended wine at the change of each season much to the pleasure of Northern Michigan tourists and wine fanciers. The results of this new blending philosophy are wines that express the freedom of creativity and good taste. These seasonal offerings have been a contributing factor in Leelanau Wine Cellars' move from the seventh largest wine production facility in the state in 1987 to the second largest in 1994.

Winemaker Bill Skolnick sees further expansion at Leelanau Wine Cellars in the area of limited vineyard-designated wines consisting of Chardonnay, Riesling, Cabernet Franc and even bottling of small batches of Cabernet Sauvignon. He has also achieved some recognition for his efforts in producing a notable port-style wine. Quite an accomplishment, in such a short time, from a winery that at one time produced more fruit wine than premium table wines.

Today, the luscious fruit wines of the peninsula are still playing a prominent role in the scheme of things, but the forty-five acres of prime vineyards up the hill from the winery offer more than a spectacular view of Grand Traverse Bay. It seems likely that more award-winning premium wine will be flowing from "them thar hills"!

Lemon Creek Vineyards

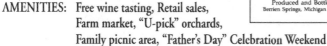

LOCATION: 533 Lemon Creek Road
Berrien Springs, MI 49103
(616) 471-1321

HOURS: Mon.- Sat. 9-6 PM, Sun. Noon-6 PM
May to December

AMENITIES: Free wine tasting, Retail sales,
Farm market, "U-pick" orchards,
Family picnic area, "Father's Day" Celebration Weekend

Nearly twenty-five years ago, the Lemon family realized that the same lake-effect climate conditions of cool springtimes and warm autumns that were beneficial to their six generation fruit-growing business were also helpful for the cultivation of grapes - it was a natural progression to extend their farming efforts to include grape-growing.

As the demand for premium wine grapes developed, so did the Lemons' vineyards expansion. It wasn't until 1984, however, that brothers Tim, Jeff and Bob Lemon decided to open their own winery and diversify their production to include the marketing of wine during the winter months. Today, Lemon Creek is still a major supplier of premium grapes to a number of Michigan wineries as well as a prominent producer of wines under its own label.

Lemon Creek's major contribution to Michigan's wine industry is their production of Vidal Blanc, a popular and versatile grape variety that has won wine awards under several winery labels, including the Lemon Creek Vineyards banner.

Lemon Creek is, first and foremost, a multiple-fruit farm. The winery is small, but it has its advantages in quality control of production. According to the Lemons, "We use only our own grapes, overseen from vineyard to bottle, by a staff comprised of family members."

The quality reputation of Lemon Creek grapes and wine has also made the farm a favorite of home winemakers from all over the Midwest. With a selection including Johannisberg Riesling, Vidal Blanc, Chambourcin, Vignoles, Seyval, Baco Noir and newly-planted Chardonnay, Gewurztraminer, Cabernet Sauvignon, Pinot Noir and Merlot, there's plenty to choose from whether it's "pick-your-own" grapes or juice straight from the crusher.

Bring the family to visit Lemon Creek (plenty of non-alcoholic fruit juices are available) and have a picnic on the grounds. In June, on Father's Day weekend, Lemon Creek hosts a festival that includes hayrides, games for the kids, arts and crafts booths and live music.

Old Mission Cellars

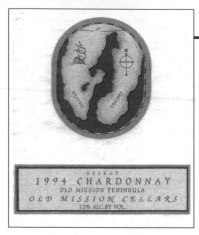

SELECT
1994 CHARDONNAY
OLD MISSION PENINSULA
OLD MISSION CELLARS
12% ALC.BY VOL.

LOCATION: Old Mission Road
            Old Mission Peninsula
            Old Mission, MI 49673
            (North of Traverse City)
            (616) 223-4310

HOURS: Mon.-Sat. Noon - 8 PM
            Sun. 12-5, Year round

AMENITIES: Free wine tasting, Retail sales

The village of Old Mission was established in 1840 on northwest Michigan's Old Mission Peninsula and is the original settlement of this popular Grand Traverse Bay area. Although the village has only contained a general store and post office for years, as of the summer of 1995 it will also be the home of Michigan's newest winery. Old Mission Cellars is the brainchild of Dave Kroupa whose great-grandfather settled in the area from Bohemia in the mid-1800's. "Our family started farming and my grandfather planted orchards", states Kroupa. The Kroupa family has over 150 acres of cherries and according to Kroupa the dwindling demand for the peninsula's number one crop over the last few years created an opportunity to plant wine grapes "to see if the farm could make a little better profit."

Kroupa has obviously been watching the growing success of the peninsula's wine industry and felt now was the time to join the ranks of the region's wine growers. Initially, Kroupa was just going to plant and farm the grapes and sell them to peninsula wineries, but after "adding everything up, it just gives us a better return on our investment to include a winery... plus it is a good outlet for our cherry juice," explains Kroupa.

As this book goes to press, Old Mission Cellars is just getting started and is fermenting some cherry and apple wine, including a very unusual yellow sweet cherry wine that is perfectly clear in color and looks like an ordinary white grape wine in the glass. Future harvests will yield Chardonnay and Riesling varieties which continue to do very well in the peninsula's temperate micro-climate due to the protection of Lake Michigan's Grand Traverse Bay on both sides.

Old Mission Cellars is currently a modest, quaint little winery with a tasting room that is located in a remote area of Michigan's Old Mission Peninsula. But Dave Kroupa accurately describes the area as "seemingly sparse when compared to the city, but here at the back of the farm, it's getting pretty crowded". Everything is relative.

Peterson and Sons Winery

LOCATION: 9375 East P Ave.
Exit 85 S off I-94
Kalamazoo, MI 49001-9762
(616) 626-9755

HOURS: Mon.- Sat. 10-6 PM,
Sun. Noon - 6 PM, Year round

AMENITIES: Free wine tasting,
Retail sales

Other than standard Cranberry Wine
Produced & Bottled by Peterson & Sons Winery
Kalamazoo, MI 49001 "Bonded Wine Cellar No. 56"
Alcohol 8 % by volume For Sale in Michigan Only

After being laid off from his regular job, Duane Peterson decided to expand his hobby of making wine. His first step was to take samples of his home-made wines to be tested by one of Michigan's larger wineries to see if they met state and federal regulations and to get a straight answer as to the feasibility of entering the commercial market with his product.

The recommendation from the winemaker was to "go for it!" That was in 1983 and since then Peterson and his sons Tony and Todd have continued to build a modestly successful winery as part of Michigan's growing wine industry. Peterson's label is called "Naturally Old Fashioned Wines" and boasts "No Chemicals or Sulfites" added during production of the wine. This claim, plus the emphasis on producing unusual fruit wines such as Rhubarb/ Cherry, Red and Black Raspberry, Cranberry/Raspberry and Wild Elderberry, has put Peterson and Sons Winery in a unique market niche.

"Basically, the old gentleman that taught me winemaking didn't use any chemicals and I wasn't smart enough to use them on my own," states Peterson. "We are unusual in that we add water and sugar to the fruit fermentation. We also ferment the whole piece of fruit; skin, pulp and seeds. There are probably only a half-dozen wineries in the world that follow this process. Our wines seem to naturally ferment to a higher alcohol content, some up to 15.5% in both the fruit and grape wines. We pay more for our fruit than many wineries, but we only want the best fruit, hand-picked into our sanitized lugs." Peterson continues, "With our style of wine and working with small fifty-five gallon batches, we just felt it wasn't necessary to use chemicals. I'm not sure why, but everything seems to work and there are more and more new customers that agree with our philosophy and old-fashioned way of making wine. I consider our method of winemaking an art form and a gift...I just don't question the results."

Rogue River Winery

LOCATION: 41 Courtland St.
(in the "Barrel Shop")
Rockford, MI 49341
(616) 866-3327
(800) 648-9860

HOURS: 10 AM to 6 PM, Mon.- Sat.
Noon to 5 PM, Sunday

AMENITIES: Tasting room,
Beer & winemaking supplies

Rogue River Winery is the smallest bonded winery in Michigan, if not in the entire Great Lakes Region. The winery, with its two or three barrels of wine, takes up very little space in the back room of the retail store called "The Barrel Shop". The winery/retail shop is located in a charming tourist shopping area called "Squires Street" in the small town of Rockford, just north of Grand Rapids.

In reality, Rogue River is little more than a home winemaking operation and an extension of the retail store. Indeed, its major business is supplying hobbyists with all the essentials for producing homemade beer and wine.

The brand new owner of Rogue River is Scott Dittenber who "just started working part-time at the shop a couple of years ago in order to save money to buy a keg system for my home, and one thing led to another." The end result is that Dittenber now owns a bonded winery license, as well as the retail outlet.

Rogue River began as a specially licensed extension tasting room for Michigan's Fenn Valley Winery in the 1980's. Eventually, the original owners started to dabble in producing hybrid and fruit wines under their Rogue River label, named after the river that winds through the downtown area.

Today, Rogue River produces and sells a cherry wine and a red hybrid table wine from fruit purchased locally. Dittenber experiments with five-gallon batches of mead, cider and various other wines at his home and would eventually "like to explore the possibility of making some Rogue River specialty wines like Sparkling Apple or Dandelion Wine. I would like to have something unusual and different that people couldn't find anywhere else," says Dittenber, "but for now, I'll be concentrating on the beer and winemaking business and we'll take things one step at a time."

In the meantime, the "old town" atmosphere of the city square is worth visiting for unique gift shopping and a free sample of Rogue River wine at the Barrel Shop's tasting bar.

St. Julian Wine Company

St.Julian®

Appellation
Lake Michigan Shore

Village Blush®

A Fine Table Wine

Proudly Produced and Bottled
by St.Julian Wine Co. Inc.
Paw Paw, Michigan U.S.A.
Bonded Winery MI-23

LOCATION: 716 S. Kalamazoo St.
Paw Paw, MI 49079
(616) 657-5568

HOURS: Mon.- Sat. 9 AM-5 PM
Sun. Noon-5 PM, Year round

AMENITIES: Free wine tasting, Eight outlets
throughout the state, Retail sales &
gift shops, Guided winery tour,
Cafe/pizzeria at the winery, Personal labeling service

Modern winemaking throughout the world is deeply embedded in family traditions. Some of those family histories expand to the "New World" and include not only California, but are also evident in the Great Lakes Region. One such family of winemakers are the Meconi's who record five generations of winemaking in Italy. The sixth generation descendant, Mariano Meconi, decided to practice his trade across the ocean and created what is now known as the St. Julian Wine Company. Two more Meconi generations have since evolved and have combined to create the largest winery in Michigan with tasting rooms in all the major tourist areas of the state.

The winery location in Paw Paw also offers a very attractive and popular Italian-style cafe or *trattoria*. Besides offering sandwiches, pizza and light entrees, *Apollo's* houses an enchanting toy museum for young and old alike.

St. Julian offers a variety of premium table wines, including Chancellor, a French-American red grape wine that has won national attention from Florida to California for its award-winning status. A rapidly expanding grape variety for St. Julian is their "Lake Michigan Shore Chardonnay". It is very unlike many of the California Chardonnays and more closely resembles those produced from cooler growing regions such as some parts of France.

St. Julian's introduction of "Michigan Raspberry Champagne" is fast becoming a marketing success story . The pronounced, racy flavor and fragrant aroma of fresh red raspberries has catapulted this delightful sparkling wine to the forefront of the taste buds of the winery's admirers.

Rounding out St. Julian's repertoire of fine wines is the nationally-acclaimed Solera Cream Sherry which many will argue is the best Cream Sherry made in this country. Since 1975 this wonderful combination of caramelized, nutty flavors has won over thirty gold medals in national and international wine judgings.

Seven Lakes Vineyard

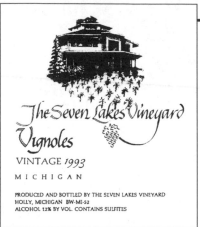

The Seven Lakes Vineyard
Vignoles

VINTAGE *1993*
M I C H I G A N

PRODUCED AND BOTTLED BY THE SEVEN LAKES VINEYARD
HOLLY, MICHIGAN BW-MI-52
ALCOHOL 12% BY VOL. CONTAINS SULFITES

LOCATION: 1111 Tinsman Road
(between Holly and Fenton)
Fenton, MI 48430
(313) 629-5686

HOURS: Wed.- Sat. 10-6 PM
Sun. Noon-6 PM
Year round

AMENITIES: Free wine tasting, Retail Sales,
Special summer winery events

In a state where most of the grape-growing attention is focused on the south-west and northwest regions, there is a quiet, maverick sort of winemaker from the land of "steel and wheels" between Flint and Detroit.

Seven Lakes Vineyard consists of twenty acres of hybrid grapes planted by Harry and Chris Guest in 1978 on farmland near Holly, MI. Winemaker Chris Guest feels that the area is probably one of the warmest grape-growing regions in the state which allows him to achieve consistently ripe fruit each year. His contention is that Lake Erie and the nearby inland lakes help keep the area warm, much like Lake Michigan does for the west side of the state. "If you track the weather charts", says Guest, "you'll find the center of the state is the coldest, on average, and it gets warmer toward both the east and west shores of the state. That's why all of Michigan's fruit crops do so well in these coastal areas."

Where most Michigan grape growers and winemakers are expanding their vineyards into the popular vinifera or "European style" grapes, Seven Lakes remains loyal to the French-American hybrid wine grapes they started with. "I think it is important that Michigan, as well as any other grape-growing region, establish its own distinctiveness within the wine market," proclaims Guest. "In the long run, we will be better off with our own identity than if we continue to try and emulate a wine or wine region that is not exposed to the same soil and climate conditions that we are given by nature. We feel the future of Seven Lakes is in developing and expanding the Vignoles grape for white wine and DeChaunac for red table wines. Our particular area is just not conducive to the successful development of Chardonnay or Riesling."

There seems to be some validity to Guest's philosophy with the success and popularity of the Seven Lakes wines. The winery has no problem selling all of its 5,000 gallon average production each year to Detroit-area restau-rants, retailers and visitors to the tasting room.

Sharon Mills Winery

LOCATION: 5701 Sharon Hollow Road
Manchester, MI 48158
(313) 428-9160

HOURS: Open Sat. & Sun. Noon to 5 PM
or by appointment, Year Round

AMENITIES: Free wine tasting, Picnic grounds,
Reception facilities

Sharon Mills Winery, located between Chelsea and Manchester in the south-central part of the state, has two claims to fame. First is their position as Michigan's only winery that produces champagne-style wines exclusively, and second is the historic building that actually houses the winery.

The building was originally built in the mid-1830's as a gristmill. In the 1900's, it was owned by Henry Ford, who rebuilt it and added a generator in 1933. That generator is still being used as a source of electrical energy for the winery. In 1960, the Hawker family purchased the property as their primary residence. Craig and Michael Hawker were raised on the site and decided in 1989 to develop the family's little piece of Michigan history into something that would be of interest and a source of enjoyment to others. After much research and deliberation with the folks at Chateau Grand Traverse in Traverse City, a winery was born.

This small, thousand-case winery sits along the River Raisin near Manchester and is often used as the perfect setting for summer weddings. A banquet room overlooking the grounds and the river is rented for not only bridal receptions, but for parties of all sorts.

The Hawkers are proud of their popular award-winning sparkling wines; Sparkling Riesling, Sparkling Chardonnay and a limited release of Rose of Sharon, a blend of 80 percent Chardonnay and 20 percent Pinot Noir. The skins of the Pinot Noir are left on the juice just long enough to add a touch of pink color to the finished product. The results have created a very pleasant sparkling wine that has achieved an impressive list of followers.

The grapes for Sharon Mills' Michigan champagnes are grown on the Old Mission Peninsula, north of Traverse City. They are crushed and sent through their first fermentation by Chateau Grand Traverse. The second fermentation and actual champagne-making procedures are then accomplished at the historic winery site of Sharon Mills. The final products are wonderful bubbling nectars of nature.

Tabor Hill Winery and Restaurant

LOCATION: 185 MT. Tabor Road
Buchanan, MI 49107
(800) 283-3363

HOURS: Mon. & Tues. 11:30-5 PM,
Wed. - Sat. 11:30 - 10 PM
Sun. Noon-9pm, Year round

RESTAURANT: Wed.-Sat. for lunch & dinner
Sunday specials 11:30 to 4pm

AMENITIES: Free wine tasting, Retail sales
& gift shop, Guided tour,
Fine dining restaurant

Imagine yourself driving through the countryside of Southwest Michigan on what appears to be a road to nowhere surrounded by rolling hills and fragrant vineyards. Then imagine coming upon a quaint and intimate little winery and restaurant nestled high on a hill overlooking vineyards and the Lake Michigan dunes beyond. That is exactly what you will see, when you find Tabor Hill, which is correctly nicknamed "The Hidden Jewel".

Established in 1968, the wines produced at Tabor Hill have won critical acclaim throughout the country. Some of the vinifera grape varieties produced here include White Riesling, Gewurztraminer, Scheurbe and Chardonnay. One should sample and savor the sparkling wine "Grand Mark". Made from a blend of Pinot Noir and Chardonnay, its easy to understand why it was a gold medal winner at the prestigious Los Angeles County Fair Wine Competition.

As one of only two winery/restaurants in the state, Tabor Hill exemplifies the philosophy that wine is a "food beverage" and consequently the winemakers have created wines to accompany foods that will enhance any dining occasion. With your first dining experience at Tabor Hill, it becomes apparent why so many people continue to make the effort to travel to this isolated location for lunch or dinner.

Chef Don Smith creates a new menu each day in order to best utilize what foods are available fresh. Guests are encouraged to begin their visit with a trip to the wine bar and gift shop where they can sample a variety of wines, including the popular Classic Demi-Sec. After this introductory session, diners may feel better prepared to order wine with confidence once they have been seated in the small, quaint dining room. With its view overlooking the countryside and vineyards this restaurant is a credit to Tabor Hill, offering the best that Michigan's agriculture has to offer in both food and wine.

Tartan Hill Winery

LOCATION: 52nd Ave.
New Era, MI 49446
(616) 861-4657

HOURS: 12-5 PM
Daily June through Labor Day

AMENITIES: Free wine tasting,
Retail sales

Tartan Gold

Oceana County White Table Wine

750 mL
contains sulfites
Grown, Produced and
bottled by
Tartan Hill Winery, Ltd.
New Era, MI   CBCW-MI-58

One of the smallest wineries in the state is located on elevated terrain between Ludington and Muskegon at New Era, Michigan. Since 1985, owner Bob Cameron has juggled two careers, as a teacher and an insurance agent, with his love for making wine.

Cameron's introduction to wine came while he was stationed with the Army in Germany. He continued his pursuit of the grape after his tour of duty and began, as do most winemakers, making wine at home. Shortly after transferring out of the Detroit school district to West Michigan, Bob was introduced to the north country's pioneer winemaker Bernie Rink on the Leclanau Peninsula. That meeting rekindled his enthusiasm and he began looking for suitable land to advance his hobby. He decided on seven acres near New Era, resting on sandy soil and high enough to be protected from extended sub-zero temperatures. The good part was that it stood in the heart of a prosperous fruit-growing region and would prove perfect for growing grapes. The catch was that the land was already utilized as peach and apple orchards and needed to be cleared, a job not appropriate for the uncommitted.

After clearing the land, Cameron experimented with over seventy different varieties of grapes as part of his search for achieving the best possible product from the area. Currently his modest annual harvest of 500 to 800 gallons produces four Tartan Hill wines: "Tartan Red" (a 50/50 blend of Foch and DeChaunac), "Tartan White"(50% Vidal, 25% Vignoles and 25% Seyval), Amber Rosé (Cayuga and "a little" Foch) and "Tartan Gold"(50% Vidal and 50% Seyval). Within the last few years Cameron has planted vines of the European vinifera variety and looks forward to future harvests of Riesling.

Virtually the entire production of Tartan Hill wine is sold at the winery tasting-room between Memorial Day and Labor Day. "Obviously, we depend quite heavily on the tourist trade to sample and buy our wines and then all the proceeds go back into the vineyard and winery," says Cameron.

Warner Vineyards

MICHIGAN
BRUT
Champagne

Naturally Fermented in this Bottle
Cellared and Bottled at the winery by Warner Vineyards
Paw Paw, Van Buren County, Michigan
Alcohol 12% by volume

LOCATION: 706 S. Kalamazoo St.
Paw Paw, MI 49079
(616) 657-3165

HOURS: Mon.-Sat. 9-6 PM
Sun. 12-6 PM
Winter hours, daily 10-5 PM

AMENITIES: Free wine tasting,
Champagne cellar tour,
Railroad car gift shop

Three generations of Warners have overseen this Michigan winemaking firm since its inception in 1938 as an adjunct to the family banking, farm-supply and farming businesses. Over the years, family members have developed a very unique and popular site. Situated on the riverbank in downtown Paw Paw, the heart of Michigan's wine country, Warner has transposed the village's old water-works building into the winery's visitors' center. This state-designated historical structure, built in 1898, is unique with its interesting architecture of an exaggerated roof line and tall, solitary chimney. Inside this unusual facade is the visitors' tasting room which also features a re-creation display of European Champagne Caves. Adjacent to the tasting-room building is an old 1914 Grand Trunk Railroad passenger rail car that serves as a popular gift shop and curiosity attraction.

Warner specializes in *méthode champenoise* sparkling wines which are carefully nurtured toward a second fermentation process within each bottle. The trapped gases of this fermentation are what give the wine its bubbles. Warner offers notable samples of brut, extra dry and sweeter spumante versions of the bubbly wine.

Through a cooperative facility lease agreement with Fenn Valley Winery and six other winemaking facilities, Warner also produces a line of French hybrid wines and seven flavorful non-alcoholic sparkling fruit juices, as well as dessert wines such as solera sherry and port. The best-selling wine in the Warner product line, called *Liebestruben*, is a blend of hybrid grapes with a touch of the Muscat grape to give it the pleasant, sweet taste of the popular German Liebfraumilch wines.

Though Warner's distribution of their products is primarily in Michigan, a significant amount of the non-alcoholic sparkling juices is shipped to the East Coast and a line of wines called "Warner West" is made and distributed on the West Coast.

NEW YORK

The State of New York is the second largest producer of grapes and wines in the United States, second only to California. New York has six officially recognized viticultural areas similar to the "appellations of origin" in France. Because of their proximity to the Great Lakes, we will deal with two of them - the Lake Erie District and the Finger Lakes District, the two that are most directly affected by the waters of the Great Lakes. As with all the great winemaking regions of the world large bodies of water are crucial elements in creating ideal "micro-climates" for growing premium grapes. These two regions combined, produce more than 90% of the state's wine production.

The history of grape growing in these regions dates back to the 1820's when a minister began producing sacramental wine for his parishioners in the hamlet of Hammondsport. The grape and wine industry flourished during the 1800's and early 1900's until the devastation of Prohibition. With repeal of the law in 1933, wineries began to cautiously make their way back into wine production.

Two European immigrants played pivotal roles in re-shaping the modern New York wine industry. In 1934, Charles Fournier, the Champagne master at Veuve Cliquot in France, came to the Finger Lakes to briefly consult for Gold Seal Vineyards and never left. Among his many major contributions to the industry was the introduction of French-American grape varieties such as Seyval Blanc and Baco Noir which were developed by French scientists in response to a devastating phylloxera (a plant louse) epidemic throughout Europe. These varieties combined hardiness in the vineyard with the sophisticated taste characteristics of European wines. They quickly became staples not only in the vineyards of New York wineries, but also throughout the Midwest and in Canada.

In 1951, at the age of 52, Dr. Konstantin Frank emigrated from Russia where he had been a vineyardist in the Ukraine. Since he had experience in growing *vitis vinifera* grapes (Riesling, Chardonnay, Pinot Noir, Cabernet Sauvignon, etc.) in a cool climate region, Frank believed the classic European wine grape varieties could be grown in the Finger Lakes as well. Together, Frank and Fournier proved to the "doubting Thomas' " of the wine industry that these delicate plants could be cultivated in New York climates and the *vinifera* revolution has continued throughout the vineyards of the Great Lakes Wine Regions.

In addition to breathtaking scenic beauty, superb quality wines have become the hallmark of Finger Lakes wineries in the last decade. The four north-to-south lakes carved by Ice Age glaciers combine with the Great Lakes to the northwest to promote soil conditions and micro-climates of temperatures that are ideal for producing premium quality grapes for elegant quality wines. Western New York is by far America's largest wine-producing region outside of California.

In 1976, the State of New York passed the "Farm Winery Act" that allowed small family farms to create wineries to assure a market for their grape crops. Before the Farm Winery Act, New York had 19 wineries, today there are nearly 100. We'll visit 51 of them.

For more information and brochures, contact:
New York Wine & Grape Foundation
350 Elm Street
Penn Yan, NY 14527
(315) 536-7442

Amberg Wine Cellars

LOCATION: On Route 5 & 20 at
Seneca Castle Road
Clifton Springs, NY 14432

HOURS: 10 AM to 6 PM, Mon.-Sat.
Noon to 6 PM, Sunday

AMENITIES: Tastings & retail shop,
Hospitality center

"Gypsy" 1993
Finger Lakes White Table Wine

The Amberg family has been in the nursery business since the 1960's and when young Eric Amberg decided he wanted to earn a degree in enology (the study of winemaking) the Amberg's expanded their family business to include vineyards and a winery.

The winery is located in the old barns of a farm established in 1795, where grapes were grown commercially from 1890 to 1930. Now the tradition has begun anew. Winemaker Eric Amberg has incorporated his wine education in California, experience working in vineyards in Germany and the research being done in New York into his expanding vineyards. One interesting grape variety is "NY65533.13" from the Geneva Experimental Station. It's so new that it doesn't even have a name yet. This experimental grape is used for blending in Amberg's proprietary wines "Gypsy" and "Pearl".

The winery's new visitors center is located down Seneca Castle Road from the winery at Route 5 & 20. The spacious "Hospitality Room" easily accommodates bus tours from the highway. A sampling of Amberg wines is graciously dispensed by Eric's wife, Debbie, sometimes accompanied by their new baby, when Mom can't get a baby-sitter.

Amberg wines include a Chardonnay *Sur-Lie* (aged on the yeast) that is finished dry and without a predominance of oak in the French style of Burgundy. A Riesling shows the winemaker's experience in Germany with a slightly sweet finish and fragrant bouquet. The third varietal wine is the red Pinot Noir which is very difficult to grow and vinify in the area, but shows nice balance and finesse. A Late-Harvest Riesling and Cabernet Sauvignon are also in the works for future release.

Besides three or four additional blended wines, the tasting room also offers an array of custom designed gift baskets for friends and relatives back home. The Amberg Wine Cellars' tasting room is easily accessible, brand new and the pride and joy of the Amberg family (next to baby Amberg, that is).

43

Americana Vineyards

LOCATION: 4367 East Covert Road
Interlaken, NY 14847-9720
(607) 387-6801

HOURS: 10 AM to 5 PM, Mon.-Sat.
Noon to 5 PM, Sunday
Weekends only, April, Nov. & Dec.
Closed Jan.-March

AMENITIES: Tasting & tours

Along the Cayuga Wine Trail via Route 89, one is surrounded by the feeling of country friendliness offered by the neighboring wineries. As the Cayuga Lake folks say, "It's a journey through tradition...and a winemaking heritage. Be part of our journey." All the wineries along the trail would be considered small in terms of production, but they are big on personal hospitality.

The one farm winery that best exemplifies the cordiality of the area is Americana Vineyards operated by Jim and Mary Anne Treble. Entering their winery tasting room is truly like walking into Americana. From the Early American decor, the wooded and vineyard scenery, the hand-crafted quilts on display and the genuine warm greetings of its owners, it's no wonder that "Big City" residents love to drive into the Finger Lakes region to escape the hustle and stress of urban life.

Jim Treble is a teacher of broadcast media at Ithaca College, but he and his wife, Mary Anne, have been home winemakers for many years and the winery is their haven for the tranquil life on weekends and during the summer. Mary Anne states that, "We used to make wine just for ourselves and our friends, but it grew to the point that we had so much wine we had to go commercial and sell it." Today, Americana Vineyards produces about 4-5,000 gallons each harvest and they sell it all. "That's where we are going to stay," says Treble, "it's just the two of us and all our kids are out doing other things, so we'll just continue at this pace and keep it enjoyable."

All of the Americana Vineyards wines are accessible only at the winery and a tour of the fermentation facilities and tasting of up to eleven wines is always available with the Treble's compliments.

Americana Vineyards Winery is a step back in time when life was simpler, friendlier and secure with the warm feeling of being back home.

Anthony Road Wine Company

LOCATION: 1225 Anthony Road
            (just off Route 14)
            Penn Yan, NY 14527
            (315) 536-2182

HOURS: 10 AM to 5 PM, Mon.-Sat.
            Noon to 5 PM, Sunday
            April to December

AMENITIES: Tasting room, Picnic area

ANTHONY ROAD

FINGER LAKES

dry white wine

Vintner's Select

VINTED AND BOTTLED BY
ANTHONY ROAD WINE COMPANY, INC., PENN YAN, NEW YORK
ALCOHOL 11.0% BY VOLUME

In the late 1970's the grape farming business in the Finger Lakes was experiencing a major transformation. Consumer tastes were changing from the grapey flavor of American juice varieties to the more traditional taste of European style wines. The giant company Taylor, who was the major buyer of grapes from area farms was feeling the pinch on business. In 1976, the New York State legislature passed a Farm Winery Act that allowed grape farmers to make wine and sell it directly to the consumer. This saved many farms, but unfortunately not the Taylor Wine company.

John and Ann Martini had been growing grapes for the Taylor company since the early 1970's and anticipated the change in the market. John discussed the situation with his friend Derek Wilber who had been a winemaker at another large winery for a number of years. Both men saw the "handwriting on the wall" and decided to pool their resources and energies to take advantage of the new state bill by starting a new winery.

John kept his full-time job as a chemist, working part-time at the winery, while Derek worked at the winery full-time. Derek's wife, Donna Ridley Wilber, maintained her job as a nurse to help support their family and John's wife, Ann, became the major force in the retail and sales end of the winery venture. Derek's brother, Andrew, has also joined the team recently and oversees the vineyard operations.

Anthony Road Wine Company offers seven wines in their line from Riesling and Chardonnay, to Seyval and Vignoles plus two blended house wines. Winemaker Derek feels that they will be emphasizing the further development of Riesling products including sparkling and reserve styles. "The market for Riesling is growing and the Finger Lakes region is proving to be an excellent area for this grape," says Derek.

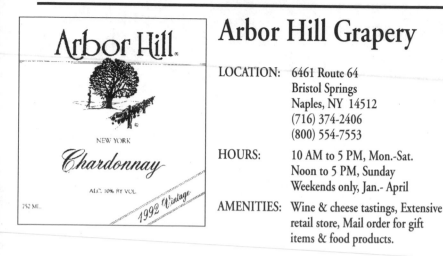

Arbor Hill Grapery

LOCATION: 6461 Route 64
Bristol Springs
Naples, NY 14512
(716) 374-2406
(800) 554-7553

HOURS: 10 AM to 5 PM, Mon.-Sat.
Noon to 5 PM, Sunday
Weekends only, Jan.- April

AMENITIES: Wine & cheese tastings, Extensive
retail store, Mail order for gift
items & food products.

Wine isn't the only delicious commodity made from grapes. And you'll never know how extensive the product line can be until you step into the Arbor Hill Grapery or leaf through the Grapery's Gift Catalog. John and Katie Braham make not only wine, but they also produce a wonderful array of wine sauces (dessert and barbecue), preserves, jellies, flavored vinegars, mustards, award-winning dressings and even the area's famous "grape pie filling." And then they put together an endless array of gift crates and custom-made baskets to be shipped to customers all over the U.S. and Canada.

The Braham's both grew up in the area and grape farming has been a part of their everyday life. John even received his degree in Pomology (the study of fruit) from Cornell University in Ithaca, New York. After spending over twenty years with Widmer's Wine Cellars, he decided to strike off on his own. The Brahams refurbished an old building that was once used as a post office, a library and a general store. Opening with the now famous Braham's Wine Sauce, they gradually developed additional products to place in the store and have grown every year since.

"I have a tendency to be an experimenter," states John, "especially in the vineyard." As vice president of vineyard operations for Widmer, Braham was able to combine his experience of growing up on a grape farm and his educational training. Now with his own vineyard operation, he continues to expand by showcasing experimental grape varieties that have since become his trademark under the Arbor Hill label. From native *Labrusca*, to French hybrid, to the classic European *Vinifera*, Braham and Arbor Hill offer a full selection of wines to satisfy any palate.

Arcadian Estate Vineyards

LOCATION: 4184 State Route 14
Rock Stream, NY 14878
(607) 535-2068

HOURS: Noon to 6 PM, Daily
Dec.-March; Fri., Sat. & Sun. only

AMENITIES: Tastings & tours, Retail shop,
Special events

Family wineries are not uncommon in the Finger Lakes, but at Arcadian Estate Vineyards the family ownership is uniquely structured. Joanne Hatrich and her brother, Charlie Langendorfer, run the day-to-day operation of the winery. Joanne works in the retail tasting room, and Charlie is the winemaker, while their respective spouses, Mike and Brigid, keep their "day jobs" to hold down the operating expenses. The two couples purchased the winery in 1993 and have worked diligently to make the venture successful. Although Joanne and Charlie are the full time employees, Mike and Brigid also keep a "killer" pace, especially during the tourist season.

Both the interior and exterior of the Arcadian Winery is typical of Finger Lakes' barn-structure wineries, but the similarity ends there. This barn is accented with four stained-glass windows recovered from an old church in the area. Inside, a large walk-around tasting bar easily accommodates visitors as they wander the room shopping for farm gift items like syrups, jellies or Joanne's homemade fabric wine bags. To commemorate the family partnership, the couples have commissioned a local artist to paint the winery's short history on tiles as well as the grape history of the Finger Lakes. The tiles will be mounted on the tasting bar for all to see.

The Arcadian Estate Winery specializes in red wine grape varieties, featuring Baco Noir, DeChaunac, Foch and new in 1995 is a Pinot Noir. White varieties include Cayuga, Riesling, Seyval and Chardonnay. These energetic couples have already more than doubled the previous owner's production from 4,000 gallons to 10,000 and it doesn't look like they're going to stop there.

Just to be sure, there's always something to do for each of the family partners. Arcadian sponsors a number of special promotions during the year in addition to participating in the events of the Seneca Lake Wine Trail. By the looks of things, there isn't going to be any moss growing on the Arcadian family partnership.

BULLY HILL
Vineyards

Summertime at the Winery

Bully Hill Vineyard
(and St. Walter de Bully Wine Co.)

LOCATION: 8843 Greyton H. Taylor Memorial Dr.
Hammondsport, NY 14840
(607) 868-3610

HOURS: 9 AM to 5 PM, Mon.-Sat.
Noon to 5 PM, Sunday

AMENITIES: Tour & tasting (on the hour),
Gift Shop, Restaurant (May-Nov.),
Museum

The story of Bully Hill Vineyards is one of the strangest in the Finger Lakes, if not in the entire industry. The saga begins in 1878 with the Taylor family's purchase of a seven acre vineyard and a cabin on a piece of land known as Bully Hill. Over the course of four generations, the Taylor family built a fledging wine business at a location down the road from the original vineyard. By 1970, the now huge Taylor Wine Company came under the control of a Board of Directors and company stockholders and Walter S. Taylor, grandson of the founder, was discharged from the firm.

Prior to his departure, Walter S. bought back the original Taylor family land and revived the property. His departure from the Taylor operation was not amicable and a feud of sorts ensued with Walter using the Taylor family name on his new venture. In 1977, Coca Cola of Atlanta purchased the large Taylor Wine Co. and sued Walter S. to prevent him from using the Taylor name. A U.S. Federal Court upheld Coca Cola's suit and Walter S. was informed he could no longer use the Taylor name in conjunction with his winery.

Since that time, Walter S. has conducted a masterful public relations and marketing campaign to tell the story of wrong-doing toward his family name while maintaining his winery under the name of Bully Hill. He's become the "champion of social injustice," taken a "politically correct" stand on issues of ecology and international trade...and sold a lot of wine. Some pretty good wine, at that.

The Taylor Wine Company has since been sold to the giant Canandagua Wine Co., but the production plant has been shut down. No matter, a visit to the Bully Hill compound is still worth a trip to the area, especially during fall color time, the view is magnificent. Plan on taking the hour tour for an entertaining day at an extraordinary winery complete with a restaurant, wine museum and a gallery with some intriguing label paintings.

48

Casa Larga Vineyards

LOCATION: 27 Emerald Hill Circle
Fairport, NY 14450
(716) 223-8899

HOURS: 10 AM to 6 PM, Mon.-Sat.
Noon to 6 PM, Sunday

AMENITIES: Tasting and tours,
Extensive gift shop,
Banquet facilities, Special events

Blanc de Blancs
Méthode Champenoise

FINGER LAKES CHAMPAGNE
PRODUCED AND BOTTLED BY CASA LARGA VINEYARDS, INC.
FAIRPORT, NEW YORK

This impressive architectural award-winning winery is a brilliant combination of old world tradition and charm with state-of-the-art technology designed for contemporary use and efficiency.

Andrew Colaruotolo (affectionately known as Mr. "C" by the staff) emigrated to the Rochester area from his native Italy and worked as a laborer while he learned the masonry trade. As he built a successful construction business he continued his hobby of winemaking. Colaruotolo's hobby evolved into a winery in 1974 and eventually into the current magnificent complex that sits atop the highest point in the county.

Colaruotolo originally planned on developing the winery's 30 acres into a housing project while he searched for vineyard land in other parts of the state. Not finding anything he liked, he had his soil tested at Cornell University and discovered it was Ontario Sandy Loam, a highly desirable soil for growing grapevines. The land was planted and Colaruotolo built executive homes around the perimeter of the vineyard to help finance the project.

The Casa Larga structure with its old-world bell tower and piazza, dramatic floor-to-ceiling windows, Italian marble and vaulted ceilings is so impressive that it is difficult to talk about anything else. But, once you enter the strikingly attractive retail room your attention is immediately diverted to an extensive array of eye-catching merchandise and wines of notable quality.

The effort Colaruotolo devoted to the construction of his illustrious building is also reflected in the quality of his wines. All the vineyards are tended by hand to produce an award-winning Chardonnay and over 100 other awards for wines that include Pinot Blanc, Vidal Blanc, Riesling, Cabernet Sauvignon, Pinot Noir and a number of estate blended wines.

"We have always felt that our winery has been a place for people to come and enjoy the building and grounds as much as the wine," says General Manager John Colaruotolo. It is worth the trip to Casa Larga Vineyards just to see the masterpiece that Mr. "C" built...and to drink his wine.

Finger Lakes   1992
**Johannisberg
Riesling**

PRODUCED AND BOTTLED BY
CASTEL GRISCH WINERY
WATKINS GLEN, NEW YORK 14891 607-535-7711
CONTAINS SULFITES   ALCOHOL 12% BY VOL.

Castel Grisch Estate Winery

LOCATION: 3380 County Route 28
Watkins Glen, NY 14891
(607) 535-9614

HOURS: 10 AM to 6 PM, Mon.-Sat.
Noon to 6 PM, Sunday

AMENITIES: Tasting room & gift shop,
Full service restaurant,
Bed & Breakfast Manor

People are one of the most attractive features of the Finger Lakes. Some come from generations of area farm families. Some come from large cities to escape the "rat race" of urban life and others leave the area where they were born only to return after they have experienced the world around them. The one attribute they all have in common is that they are just "nice folks" and they make you feel right at home.

This warm, friendly feeling is very prevalent at the Castel Grisch Estate, situated on a high slope overlooking Watkins Glen and the southern end of Seneca Lake. Tom and Barbara Malina purchased the estate in 1992 from a Swiss family who developed the location because of its similarities to their native Switzerland. Barbara was raised in the area and knew the property well. Her husband, Tom, was in the wine and liquor import business for a large international firm. They decided to return to Watkins Glen and operate the winery, restaurant and Bed & Breakfast Manor.

The continental ambiance of the estate was preserved by the Malina's and they have trained their staff well to carry on the founders' European traditions of fine estate-produced wines, tastefully distinct cuisine and elegant overnight accommodations. The scenic hillside estate is truly a celebration of wine, food and friends all blended together to enhance the pleasure of their guests. The Castel is the ideal spot for wedding receptions, private parties, corporate meetings and family gatherings, not to mention a great meal for two in the Swiss chalet decor of the restaurant.

Barbara and Tom Malina are gracious hosts who enjoy being part of their guests' "good life." That good life includes occassional seven course/seven wine gourmet dinners and an Oktoberfest celebration the last weekend in October, as well as other Seneca Lake Wine Trail events. Excellent limited production/estate bottled wines, a romantic room and superb apple strudel...what else is there in life?

Cayuga Ridge Estate

CAYUGA RIDGE
ESTATE

Cellar Reserve

1991
CHANCELLOR
APPELLATION CAYUGA LAKE

ESTATE GROWN AND BOTTLED BY
CAYUGA RIDGE ESTATE VINEYARD
OVID, NEW YORK
TABLE WINE • CONTAINS SULFITES

LOCATION: 6800 Route 89
            Ovid, NY 14521
            (607) 869-5158

HOURS: Noon to 5 PM, Daily
            Dec.- May, Sat. & Sun Only
            Noon to 4 PM

AMENITIES: Tastings & tours, Picnic facilities

Tom Challen spent twenty years in the winery business in Ontario before he found a 35 acre farm on Cayuga Lake. His experience told him that grapes would thrive in the chalk soils and the micro-climate created by the gently sloping topography and open waters of Cayuga Lake. He knew these were perfect conditions for developing the subtle character of the Riesling grape, the variety he knew so well from its success on the Niagara Peninsula in Canada.

Challen also became aware that the first commercial planting of the newly developed hybrid Cayuga grape was planted in the area by the New York State Agricultural Experiment Station in Geneva. He reasoned that with all the research and effort put into the project's location, this farm, which sat right in the middle of the undertaking, would be his golden opportunity for success with both grapes.

In May of 1991, Tom and Susan Challen became the proud owners of Cayuga Ridge Estate. They have since expanded their grape crop to include Chardonnay, Pinot Noir, and the French hybrid Chancellor. They converted a big, old red barn into a charming, rustic tasting room and gift shop. During the summer months the barn, the wine cellar beneath it and the deck out front are hotbeds of visitor activity. "Pinot" the peacock is the official greeter as guests enter directly off Route 89. Pinot is an unexpected attraction for winery route visitors who take the time for a picnic break at Cayuga Ridge.

Cayuga Ridge Estate is also home to the Quatrefoil (as seen on the label) Wine Society, comprised of individuals who enjoy good wine and receive member benefits, and to the Cayuga Vignerons who lease, tend and harvest fruits of their labor from their own vines at the winery. Cayuga Ridge Estate also supplies area wineries and home winemakers with their distinctive grapes and juices.

The Challens have enjoyed the success they sought with their Cayuga Ridge Estate and feel confident they have made the right move toward a prosperous future. We agree.

51

Chateau Lafayette Reneau

LOCATION:	Route 414
	Hector, NY 14841
	(607) 546-2062
HOURS:	10 AM to 6 PM, Mon.-Sat.
	Noon to 6 PM, Sunday
AMENITIES:	Tastings & tours,
	Extensive gift shop,
	Bed & Breakfast Inn,
	Group haywagon tours

Throughout the entire Finger Lakes area there are spectacular views of the lakes and countryside, but few wineries present the scenery in as many ways as does Chateau Lafayette Reneau. From the property of Chateau Lafayette Reneau you can picnic under their picturesque grape arbor or on their large deck, take a charming haywagon tour of the vineyards or stay the night and dine overlooking a breathtaking sunset panorama from the romantic Inn at Chateau Lafayette Reneau. Owners Dick and Betty Reno have captured the beauty of Seneca Lake and have packaged it for the maximum enjoyment of their guests.

A tour of the Finger Lakes would not be complete without a stop at the Chateau. The winery is housed in a three-tiered building on the side of a slope. Entering from the parking lot places you on the top level of the tasting room and gift shop. While taking the winery tour you'll descend to the storage tank area and then to the lower level of the actual winery operations containing the presses, fermentation tanks and bottling facilities. Then it's back to the top level for wine tasting and shopping in an intriguing shop containing antiques, collectibles, gourmet food products and a wide variety of wine-related gift items. A perfect package to accompany the popular selection of Chateau Lafayette Reneau wines that range from Cabernet to Chardonnay plus dry, semi-sweet and late harvest versions of Riesling.

If you're not staying at one of the Inn's ten meticulously renovated rooms in the 1911 farmhouse, then be sure to plan a picnic lunch on the deck and enjoy the view with a bottle of fine Chateau Lafayette Reneau wine. The Reno's put it best as they invite you to visit because "it is more than just another trip to a winery. It's a mini-vacation, a respite from stress." And don't forget to bring your camera!

Dr. Frank's Vinifera Wine Cellars

(and Chateau Frank Champagne Cellars)

LOCATION: 9749 Middle Rd.
Hammondsport, NY 14840
(607) 868-4884

HOURS: 9 AM to 5 PM, Mon.-Sat.
Noon to 5 PM, Sunday

AMENITIES: Tasting & retail room

D̲r. Konstantin Frank is a legend in the annals of grapegrowing and winemaking in the Eastern United States. It was Dr. Frank who proved that the classic European *Vinifera* grape varieties could be grown in that colder climate and he opened a whole new era for American winemaking.

Dr. Frank emigrated to New York State from the Ukraine in 1951, after his 50th birthday. At first he was considered somewhat of an agitator by claiming he could make the *Vinifera* varieties prosper in the Finger Lakes area because he did it in the Ukraine and the climate was more severe there than in the region that is tempered by the Great Lakes. In 1962, he introduced the first New York State *Vinifera* wine and the rest of the story has become the history of eastern grape-growing that continues to expand with every growing season.

Dr. Frank's Vinifera Wine Cellars is now in the capable hands of son, Willy, and grandson, Fred. Willy was somewhat of a rebel like his father when he decided the company should produce champagne-style wines as well as their famous white table wines. Dr. Frank was not in agreement, so Willy bought the building next door and opened Chateau Frank Champagne Cellars on his own. The Brut Champagne and Célèbre wines have become renowned for their distinctive style and clean European taste. Another Frank was right.

The fact that their winery is still family owned, free of investors who are trying to maximize profits, enables the Frank's to continue the quality winemaking that Dr. Konstantin Frank dedicated his life to.

Dr. Frank's Vinifera Wine Cellars' tasting room is not the best merchandised or the fanciest one you'll come across in the Finger Lakes, but if you have any interest at all in the history of premium wine and want to taste some of the best wine east of the California border, then you must pay a visit to the Vinifera Wine Cellars.

BARRY

NEW YORK STATE

Niagara

A medium-dry, fruity white table wine

ALCOHOL 11% BY VOLUME
PRODUCED AND BOTTLED BY EAGLE CREST VINEYARDS, INC.
CONESUS, NEW YORK 14435   BW-NY-686

GOVERNMENT WARNING: (1) ACCORDING TO THE SURGEON GENERAL, WOMEN SHOULD NOT DRINK ALCOHOLIC BEVERAGES DURING PREGNANCY BECAUSE OF THE RISK OF BIRTH DEFECTS. (2) CONSUMPTION OF ALCOHOLIC BEVERAGES IMPAIRS YOUR ABILITY TO DRIVE A CAR OR OPERATE MACHINERY, AND MAY CAUSE HEALTH PROBLEMS.

CONTAINS SULFITES

Eagle Crest Vineyards
(d.b.a, Barry Wine)

LOCATION: 7107 Vineyard Road
            Conesus, NY 14435
            (716) 346-2321

HOURS: 9 AM to 5 PM, Mon. - Fri.

AMENITIES: Tasting room,
            Group tours by appointment

Eagle Crest Vineyards was founded in 1872 for the specific intent of making "sacramental" wine for the clergy. The winery's original name was O-Neh-Da, which is the Seneca Indian word for hemlock. Bishop Bernard MacQuaide, the first bishop of the Rochester, New York Catholic Diocese, was the leading proponent in the establishment of the winery for the sole purpose of supplying churches with low alcohol wine to use during religious services celebrating the "Last Supper." The winery license was granted and the winery has continued to fill this specialty niche in the industry.

The Bishop's project was limited to making only sacramental wine that, to this day, is sold to clergy for religious use. Catholic, Lutheran, Episcopal and various Orthodox churches from all over the U.S. are supplied with over 15,000 cases of the Concord and Niagara based red, white and rosé wines from Eagle Crest Vineyards.

The winery does, however, bottle beverage wines under the Barry label that are allowed by law to be sold out of the retail room and at a few local package liquor stores. But over 90% of the wine produced at Eagle Crest is still designated for "sacramental use only."

The Barry table wines are made from the same native American (*Labrusca*) grape varieties as the sacramental wines. The Eastern New York area has an extensive history of growing the Labrusca varieties which are used primarily in the production of grape juice made famous by the Welsh's people. The surrounding lake-effect climate and the soils have long been regarded as some of the best fruit-growing conditions in North America.

The good Bishop saw the opportunity to utilize the "fruit of the land" to fill a need both temporal and spiritual. Group tours of the Eagle Crest facilities are available with advance appointments, but...don't expect any miracles.

Earle Estates Meadery

EARLE ESTATES MEADERY

HONEY ♥ MEAD

MOTHER
NATURES
NECTAR

A WINE
MADE FROM
PURE HONEY

CONTEMPORARY
PRODUCED & BOTTLED BY EARLE ESTATES MEADERY
RD1 Box 246, Tucker Hill Rd., Locke, N.Y. 13092
Alcohol 13.3% By Volume   Contains Sulfites

LOCATION: Tucker Hill Road
              Locke, NY 13092
              (607) 898-5940

HOURS: 10 AM to 5 PM, Wed.-Sat.
              Noon to 5 PM, Sunday

AMENITIES: Tasting & retail room,
              Tours & video presentation,
              Operational beehive display

One of the most fascinating and educational tasting rooms in the Finger Lakes is located at the Earle Estates Meadery near Cayuga Lake. Here, John and Esther Earle make, sell and explain mead. Mead is the term used for honey wine. It dates back through antiquity with historical references in Greek, Hindu, Roman and British cultures and mentions in Viking tales. Mead has long been associated with revelry and romance and is considered by some cultures to be the staff of life.

Traditional mead was made by boiling the honey to remove the pectin and protein. The outcome was a bitter liquid. Producers would add sugar to mask the harshness, but it then became very sweet. Contemporary mead is made by the Earle's using a filtering technique called "ultrafiltration." This special filtering does not use heat and the result is a crystal-clear wine that is light and delicate.

"Many customers have compared our Dry Mead to Chardonnay and our Sweet Mead to a late-harvest dessert wine," says Esther Earle. "People are amazed at how much the mead tastes like grape wine." Mead is made by fermenting pure honey, water, malt and yeast. The end product, at least at the Earle Meadery, is a refreshing wine beverage that is not heavy, cloying sweet or harsh.

Earle Estates Meadery is the result of a hobby that got out of control. From John's single beehive purchased in 1980, he now tends more than 800 colonies of bees. With the growth of honey production, the family needed to find other avenues of revenue to disperse the honey. Since John had also been an amateur winemaker for a number of years, the production of mead was a logical choice.

The tasting room of the Earle Estates Meadery has a live, working beehive on display (enclosed in glass with a private outside entrance for its flying residents) where kids and parents can observe the fantastic goings-on of a busy bee colony. A "must see" experience.

Four Chimneys Farm Winery

LOCATION: 211 Hall Road
             Himrod, NY 14842
             (607) 243-7502

HOURS: 10 AM to 6 PM, Mon. - Sat.
             Noon to 6 PM, Sunday

AMENITIES: Tasting room

In this world of highly competitive marketing, everyone is looking for that little "niche" or "hook" to get the consumer's attention. At the Four Chimneys Farm Winery, named for the four distinctive chimneys on their old Victorian farmhouse, the marketing position is to emphasize that the winery and farm are completely organic. The Four Chimneys "Community" (made up of three families) is quite innovative and unique in their growing methods in order to maintain quality grapes that produce some pleasant tasting wines.

Walter Pedersen and his wife, Dayle, started out in 1976 to establish an organic farm. "The one we found just happened to have grapes on it. If there were grain fields," Pedersen laughs, "we might have started a microbrewery instead." In the beginning, the Pedersen's knew nothing of winemaking and educated themselves with books and a lot of questions. "We traveled to Germany and France where organic wines have been produced for some time," says Walter, "and we received a lot of support from many friendly and helpful people."

The Four Chimneys Farm Winery produces wine that is completely free of chemical additives. "Of course, all wine contains sulfites," Walter adds, and goes on to explain that sulfites are a by-product of fermentation and are increased by some winemakers who add sulfur dioxide to prevent spoilage and to keep wine from oxidizing and turning brown during the harvest time. "But organic winemakers don't add any. Consequently, organic wine is very low in sulfites," says Pedersen.

Organic winemaking has its followers as witnessed in the tasting room of the old converted barn on the Four Chimneys' farm. Folks were buying "Kingdom White", "Eye of the Dove" and "Coronation" (America's first organic champagne) as well as a variety of other dry, semi-dry and sweet grape and fruit wines. There is even a series of "cooking wines" made with organic soy sauce, organic garlic (salt-free) or organic red pepper (also salt-free). Now, that's really finding a marketing niche and making the best of it.

Fox Run Vineyards

LOCATION: 670 Route 14
Pen Yan, NY 14527
(315) 536-4616

HOURS: 10 AM to 6 PM, Mon.-Sat.
11 AM to 6 PM, Sunday

AMENITIES: Tastings & tours,
Extensive gift shop,
Annual Garlic Festival, Newsletter

FOX RUN

VINEYARDS

Arctic Fox

Finger Lakes White Table Wine

Produced and bottled by Fox Run Vineyards Inc., Penn Yan, N.Y. 14527
750 ml • Alcohol 12% by volume

Scott Osborn, owner of Fox Run Vineyards, has worked from California to New York as a winemaker, cellarmaster, wine salesman, wine consultant and teacher. He has been described as a *bon vivant* who loves fine wine and food. Osborn also has a soft spot in his heart for animals as evidenced by the winery's adoption and fund-raising efforts for the Arctic Fox habitat at Rochester's Seneca Park Zoo. By all accounts, a man of this experience, compassion and zest for life, has to make good wine. Well, he does!

The *méthode champenoise* Chardonnay is an early sellout annually. The Fox Run Riesling is also a popular item in the tasting room and the blended wines are difficult to keep on the shelf. Osborn credits his location high on the Torrey Ridge overlooking Seneca Lake as providing the perfect grapegrowing soil and temperate climate that help make his wines award-winners.

Due to the popularity of Fox Run wines and the need to increase production to meet the demand, the winery has initiated an aggressive planting schedule to expand the vineyards. Beyond enlarging his sparkling wine output, Osborn wants to ultimately make a Bordeaux-style red wine using Cabernet Franc, Merlot and Cabernet Sauvignon. All these grape vines are already planted or are about to be. This would be a major accomplishment in the Finger Lakes for Fox Run.

The Fox Run winery and tasting room were recently remodeled and built around an old dairy barn. Complimentary tours take visitors throughout the building and into the vineyards, then back to the tasting bar and a dramatic view of Seneca Lake. If you've been looking for unusual wine-related items, here is where you'll find them. Fox Run has one of the most extensive gift shops in the Finger Lakes with an array of items ranging from gourmet food products to grape-covered boxer shorts. Now is that unique enough for you?

Frederick S. Johnson Vineyards

LOCATION:	West Main Road (Route 20)
	Westfield, NY 14787
	(716) 326-2191
HOURS:	10 AM to 6 PM, Daily
AMENITIES:	Tasting room

The wineries along the east coast of Lake Erie in western New York State all have the advantages of being small, family farm wineries located right on the site of their vineyards. As "estate" wineries (wineries that use only grapes that are grown on their own adjacent property) the winemakers have the opportunity to directly supervise the cultivation and harvest of the grapes for optimum results.

Grapes have been grown on the Johnson Estate for over a century and all of the grapes used to produce their wines are grown within 3000 feet of the winery. The facility is small, so the limited production (12-15,000 cases) is easily and carefully scrutinized from vineyard to bottle by the Johnson family which proudly displays the words "Estate Grown, Vinified & Bottled" on their labels. They are also the oldest "exclusively estate farm winery" in New York State.

The Johnson Estate wines include the American varieties of Delaware, Concord and Niagara as well as the French hybrid Vidal Blanc, Seyval Blanc and Chancellor Noir. A specialty wine of the winery is a rich, fruity, semi-sweet wine called *Liebeströpfchen* or "Little Love Drops". The wine is made of 100% Delaware grapes and although it is too sweet for dinner it serves well with fruit, dessert or by itself.

The Chancellor Noir is an excellent red hybrid variety that was developed in France and nearly 100,000 acres of its vines are still in production there. Chancellor produces a dark, rich table wine that ages nicely and compliments food. It is susceptible to mildew disease, however, and dry air drainage is a necessity. The favorable lake breezes that blow over the Johnson Estate make it the perfect area to grow this rewarding grape.

To learn more about the Johnson Estate land, grapes and wines, just stop by the tasting room, pick up a bottle of Johnson Estate wine and read the informative label. You'll find everything you want to know on the label... and then some.

Frontenac Point Vineyard

LOCATION: 9501 Route 89
Trumansburg, NY 14886
(607) 387-9619

HOURS: 10 AM to 4 PM, Fri. & Sat.
Noon to 4 PM, Sunday
April to December

AMENITIES: Tasting room

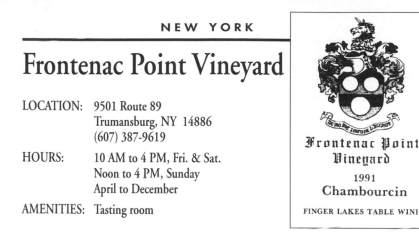

Frontenac Point
Vineyard
1991
Chambourcin
FINGER LAKES TABLE WINE

Highway 89 is the Cayuga Wine Trail. Although the area is rural, the highway is very comfortable to travel and the green grape cluster signs along the way make it easy to spot the Cayuga Lake wineries with their beautiful views of the Lake.

One such scenic spot is the Frontenac Point Vineyard located on the western shore of Cayuga Lake just 12 miles north of Ithaca, New York. Proprietors Jim and Carol Doolittle have created a classic French setting in their winery tasting room and offer estate-grown wines... "in the French tradition of winemaking."

The wine list consists of wines made from both classical European varieties (Chardonnay, Riesling and Pinot Noir) as well as French hybrids (Seyval, Vidal, Vignoles and Chambourcin). All of these varieties grow well in this region noted for its production of quality fruit . The vines are tended on slopes of low elevation, protected by a micro-climate which is the result of the influence of both Lake Ontario and Cayuga Lake.

Frontenac Point Vineyard folks say all of their wines are produced by barrel fermentation, a vinification technique that complements wines with subtlety and complexity. They then age the wine in small oak barrels of both American and European origin until mature and ready for bottling. The results are very intriguing.

Of particular interest is Chateau Doolittle, a blush wine made by blending Chardonnay with Seyval and introducing a small amount of the black grape Chambourcin. The Chambourcin (a French hybrid grape) adds the delicate color and hints of raspberry with cranberry bouquet.

Another unique wine is the Blanc de Blanc Reserve which combines Riesling, with Vidal and Vignoles then aged for 22 months in oak. The Brut Sparkling has the more classic dry finish of a Chardonnay-based wine.

Frontenac Point Vineyard's synthesis of soil, climate, grape variety and winemaking technique brings you wines which are distinctly "Appellation Finger Lakes."

Fulkerson's Winery and Juice Plant

LOCATION: 5576 Route 14
Dundee, NY 14837
(607) 243-8270

HOURS: 10 AM to 5 PM, Mon.-Sat.
Noon to 5 PM, Sunday
Memorial Day to Dec. 1

AMENITIES: Tastings & tour, Farm Market,
Home winemaking supplies

As indicated by it's name, Fulkerson's Winery and Juice Plant is a slightly different kind of winery than you'll find along the Seneca Lake Winery Trail. As you drive up to Fulkerson's it looks very much like a country farm market. Well, it is. A farm market and a winery, as well. A winery that really caters to the home winemaker more than to the walk-in retail wine trade.

Fulkerson's has been a family farm since 1805 and they established the winery in 1988. Home winemakers have become so dependent on them, however, that their business never made the complete transition to a tourist-oriented retail winery. The Fulkerson brochure, in fact, headlines "Join the many people who enjoy home winemaking and find out how rewarding and satisfying it is!" It goes on to explain that the law allows individuals to make up to 200 gallons of wine per year at home and that most people make wine in 5 gallon lots, enough to make two cases at about $1 per bottle.

Fulkerson's takes home winemaking service even one step further by offering free instructions (lessons during the season on Saturdays) and advice (free anytime) to help customers make their own wines. Over 25 varieties of fresh grape juice are available in bulk during the harvest months of September and October. Winemaking supplies and equipment (except juice and grapes) are shipped anywhere in the U.S.

Fulkerson's is an interesting stop along the Wine Trail, especially during harvest time, if for no other reason than just to see the juice plant in operation. While there, one can also try the wines of Sayre and Nancy Fulkerson and take home some fresh farm produce as well.

Glenora Wine Cellars

LOCATION: 5435 Route 14
             Dundee, NY 14837
             (607) 243-5511

HOURS: 10 AM to 5 PM, Mon.-Sat.
             11 AM to 5 PM, Sunday

AMENITIES: Tasting & tour, Video presentation,
             Special Events, Wine Garden Cafe

There are a number of reasons why visitors to the Finger Lakes should not miss visiting the impressive Glenora Wine Cellars. First and foremost is the winery's emphasis on *méthode champenoise* (fermented in the bottle) sparkling wines. Glenora hand-crafts these wines in the French tradition using only the classic varieties of Pinot Noir, Pinot Blanc and Chardonnay. Winemaker David Munksgard, who for ten years was the assistant winemaker for sparkling wines at California's Chateau St. Jean, believes the Finger Lakes' climate is "far better suited for the making of sparkling wines than most areas of California." Not only is Glenora the largest producer of *méthode champenoise* wines in the Eastern United States, but they have also gained recognition in national and international competitions for their accomplishments and are on the brink of establishing themselves as a world-class winery.

A second reason to visit Glenora is the Wine Garden Cafe with a delicious array of luncheon and dinner entrees served on the covered patio just outside the tasting room. Visitors and locals alike fill the popular cafe every day during the summer season. It's worth the effort to call ahead and reserve your table. The food and the view tempts one to stay around until the next meal.

The final reason (as if you needed more) to visit the Glenora Wine Cellars and Garden Cafe is for the number of special events that are sponsored by the winery in their outdoor pavilion. Jazz concerts, a Lobster Festival and a German Festival are just a few of the popular activities that keep people coming back to the winery.

Glenora has a handsome visitors center with an attractive tasting room, contemporary gifts and an informative video presentation that takes you on a fascinating journey from vine to wineglass. And then it's to the tasting bar to sample the superbly crafted wines of Chardonnay, Riesling, Gewürztraminer Pinot Noir, Merlot and Cabernet Sauvignon, to name a few. If you're not impressed with your visit to Glenora, then "you're a better man than I, Charlie Brown."

Hazlitt 1852 Vineyards

LOCATION:	Route 414
	Hector, NY 14841
	(607) 546-WINE
HOURS:	10 AM to 6 PM, Mon.-Sat.
	Noon to 6 PM, Sunday
	Noon to 5 PM, Fri.-Sun
	(Jan.- March)
AMENITIES:	Tasting room, Picnic facilities

The Hazlitt family settled on their current farmland in 1852 and now the fifth and sixth generations of Hazlitts continue the family tradition of grape farming. The early generations of Hazlitts produced mainly table grapes that were transported by horse-drawn wagons, steamships and railroad cars to large city markets until the 1940's when the juice and wine market developed in nearby Hammondsport. There was steady growth in this market until the bottom fell out in the mid-1970's. It was at this point that Jerry Hazlitt had to find new sources of revenue or be forced out of farming. He chose to open a winery and now the sixth generation Hazlitt is able to practice the craft of winemaking on the family farm.

The Hazlitt's large tasting room is rustic and overflowing with antique farm tools, American Indian artifacts and murals plus memorabilia from Hazlitt generations gone by. It is a popular stop along the Seneca Lake Wine Trail with visitors milling around a horseshoe-shaped tasting bar, expertly crafted from wood grown on the property. The smell of popcorn permeates the air in place of the usual fermentation aroma of wine. The constantly popping snack has become a popular trademark feature of the tasting room.

The congenial staff, which often includes one of the Hazlitts, offers samplings of a wide variety of Hazlitt wines that cover the complete gamut of native American, hybrid and *vinifera* grape varieties. From Pinot Noir to "Red Cat," from Chardonnay to "Cabin Fever" there is sure to be a wine taste to fit most every palate.

During the Christmas season the winery takes on a different air as folks gather around the warmth of a restored old wood stove. Hand-pruned Douglas Fir trees produced on the farm's Christmas tree plantation are also available for purchase.

From pine tree scent, to the enticing aroma of popcorn and the pleasing bouquet of wine, you can't get much more variety than at the Hazlitt 1852 Vineyards.

Hermann J. Wiemer Vineyard

Hermann J. Wiemer
FINGER LAKES
Johannisberg Riesling
Dry
1992

PRODUCED AND BOTTLED BY
Hermann J. Wiemer Vineyard, Inc., Dundee, N.Y.
ALCOHOL 11.5% BY VOLUME

LOCATION: Route 14
Dundee, NY 14837
(607) 243-7971

HOURS: 10 AM to 5 PM, Mon.-Sat.
11 AM to 5 PM, Sunday
Sat. & Sun. by appointment April-Nov.

AMENITIES: Tastings & tours

The winemaking industry is known for the distinctive personalities of its principals. Dealing with nature requires a strong will and determination in the face of possible disaster each year. This is particularly true in the northern growing regions where Mother Nature can be harsh and unforgiving. It takes an individual of conviction to withstand the challenges of the land.

One such individual is Hermann J. Wiemer who was born in the wine region of Bernkastel, Germany to a family with over 300 years experience in making world-renowned wines from the Mosel Valley. Wiemer arrived in the U.S. in 1968 going to work for another dominant Finger Lakes personality, Walter S. Taylor at the Bully Hill Vineyards. At Bully Hill, Wiemer learned to work with hybrid grapes which were thought to be the most equitable wine varieties to use in the Finger Lakes region.

In the mid-1970's Wiemer opened his own winery and decided that certain classic European grape varieties could prosper in the Finger Lakes microclimates and would consequently make better wine. Except for the harsher winters, he felt the weather from spring through fall was better suited for grapegrowing than his native land. It was just a matter of matching the right varieties to the right growing conditions. To do that Wiemer established a nursery to develop plant varieties and rootstock. His nursery has since become one of the major suppliers of *vinifera* grapevine cuttings for expansion and replacement vineyards in North and South America.

At the winery Wiemer now produces only the *vinifera* varieties of Chardonnay, Riesling and Pinot Noir. Wiemer also produces a critically acclaimed champagne in the traditional *méthode champenoise* style using Chardonnay and Pinot Noir grapes.

A visit to the Hermann J. Wiemer Vineyard tasting room may also include a vineyard walk through the six-acre nursery and a look at the striking architecture of the barn winery.

Heron Hill Vineyards

LOCATION: 8203 Pleasant Valley Road
Hammondsport, NY 14840
(607) 868-4241

HOURS: 10 AM to 5 PM, Mon.-Sat.
Noon to 5 PM, Sunday
Call for winter hours

AMENITIES: Tasting & retail room,
Picnic area

Heron Hill Vineyards has a unique claim to fame for their small farm winery. From 1977 to 1985 the Heron Hill Johannisberg Riesling won nine consecutive gold medals for each vintage. According to the winery's staff, no other winery in America has ever done that. Obviously, the specialty of Heron Hill is the Riesling grape variety which thrives in the Finger Lakes region of moist, cool spring weather, moderately warm summers, dry, cool autumns and the high sloping vineyard site overlooking Keuka Lake.

Because of the cool micro-climate, Heron Hill has specialized in the production of white table wines such as Riesling, Chardonnay and an assortment of other white varietals and blends. The wines all finish dry with a refreshing crispness that complements seafood and chicken. Two late harvest wines from Riesling and Muscat are also produced in a sweet, dessert style.

Peter Johnstone and John Ingle were both grape-growers prior to the New York Farm Winery Act and formed a partnership in 1977 that created Heron Hill Vineyards, Inc. The partners take a real family approach to the winery, right down to designing their marketing brochure to resemble a family album with pictures of the employees and some "homey" quotes about each of them. The friendliness of the staff carries into the tasting room and visitors are cordially treated to a lovely hillside view of the lake and some excellent white wines.

Heron Hill Vineyards is a worthwhile stop along the Keuka Lake Winery Route during the area association's seasonal activities from the Festival of Flowers and Barrel Tasting through the Harvest Festival. More information on Keuka Lake Winery Route events can be obtained by calling (315) 595-2812.

By the way, there are indeed actual herons in the vicinity of Heron Hill Vineyards. You may even be able to spot one from the winery's deck.

Hosmer Winery

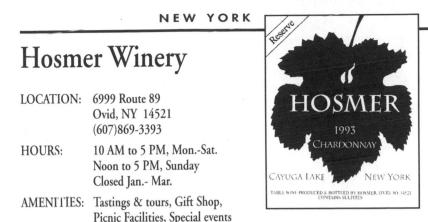

LOCATION: 6999 Route 89
            Ovid, NY 14521
            (607)869-3393

HOURS: 10 AM to 5 PM, Mon.-Sat.
            Noon to 5 PM, Sunday
            Closed Jan.- Mar.

AMENITIES: Tastings & tours, Gift Shop,
            Picnic Facilities, Special events

The Hosmer Winery is another example of a long list of New York family farms that utilized the opportunity created by the state's Farm Winery Act. The Hosmer family had been grape-growers for a number of years before they decided to open their own winery operation in 1985. Like many of the other family growers who expanded their business, the Hosmers built an attractive winery and retail building on the property to attract tourists and regular customers.

Here is where the Hosmer enterprise is set apart. Cameron and Maren Hosmer are savvy retail merchandisers. This is not common among farm growers whose main concern is tilling the soil, tending the crop and creating a quality wine product. The Hosmers do this as well on their 40 acres of vineyards, but when you walk into their retail room the initial impression is that the place is larger than a 2-3,000 case winery. In addition to a spacious tasting room, there is a mezzanine full of gourmet foods, wine paraphernalia and wine-related gifts of all sorts. It is very difficult to leave the Hosmer store without a unique gift for someone or a treat for yourself.

Hosmer Winery produces small amounts of estate bottled wines that include Chardonnay, Riesling, Cabernet Franc, Seyval, Cayuga, a selection of blended proprietary wines and a specialty dessert wine called "Raspberry Rhapsody." The Hosmer Dry Riesling at $8.00 is a tasting room favorite. However, by the looks of the packages leaving the shop, Hosmer doesn't seem to have much trouble selling everything they make.

Throughout the summer and harvest seasons, the Hosmers also host a number of special events that include barbecues, wine & food feasts and barrel tastings. With picnic facilities available you can create your own special event by purchasing some light foods and a bottle of wine from the tasting room and enjoying the scenery outdoors. Suffice it to say that the Hosmer Winery has a lot more to offer than just wine.

Hunt Country Vineyards

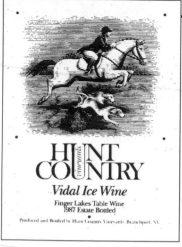

Vidal Ice Wine
Finger Lakes Table Wine
1987 Estate Bottled

Produced and Bottled by Hunt Country Vineyards, Branchport, NY.

LOCATION:	4021 Italy Hill Road
	Branchport, NY 14418
	(315) 595-2821
HOURS:	10 AM to 6 PM, Mon.-Sat.
	Noon to 6 PM, Sunday
	Closed Jan.- March
AMENITIES:	Tasting & Tours, Gift shop,
	Picnic area

In the early 1800's Aaron Hunt came to Yates County and purchased farmland on Keuka Lake near Branchport, New York. In 1973 Arthur and Joyce Hunt moved to the farm and became the sixth generation of Hunt's to work the same land. "We didn't start the winery for the romance of it, but hopefully as a way to make a living," said Hunt, who has three children. "I felt the responsibility to try to keep the farm viable for another generation. And the farm winery appeard to be a way to do that."

The winery was something of a necessity. Back in 1973 when Hunt took over the farm from his uncle, grapes where fetching $440 a ton and life was grand. But by the mid-1980's the purchase price of grapes was down as low as $80 a ton and suddenly a farm crisis raised its ugly head. At that time, many farms were consolidating or going out of business. Hunt decided to take advantage of the 1976 Farm Winery Act and build a winery. The new state law reduced fees, relaxed regulations and allowed the "farm winery" to make and sell up to 150,000 gallons a year directly to consumers and retailers.

To make the winery concept work, the Hunt's knew they had to expand their variety of grapes grown. In place of the area's traditional native American varieties the Hunt's planted *vinifera* and French hybrids. Today, their Chardonnay, Vidal Ice Wine and others are achieving the success the Hunt's were seeking. Visitors now arrive by the thousands each summer and bring picnic baskets, bicycles and hiking shoes to take advantage of the scenic trails of the area after their visit to the winery and its retail store.

One of the most popular attractions at Hunt Country Vineyards is their annual Gourmet Harvest Festival the first weekend in October. It's a great family outing with fantastic gourmet food prepared by culinary students, horse-drawn hayrides, pony rides, arts & crafts, a petting zoo and, of course, excellent Hunt Country wine.

Keuka Spring Vineyards

LOCATION: 273 East Lake Road
(Route 54)
Penn Yan, NY 14527

HOURS: Summer: 10:30 AM to 5 PM,
Mon.-Sat.
Noon to 5 PM, Sun.
May/June, Sept.- Nov. -
Weekends only

AMENITIES: Tastings, Gift shop, Picnic area

Judy and Len Wiltberger are typical of the involved, working couples prevalent in the Finger Lakes wine business. Len works at Kodak and is winemaker for Keuka Spring evenings, weekends and in his spare time. Judy is president of the Keuka Lake Winery Association and guides the planning efforts for the annual Winery Route activities.

The Keuka Lake events start in April with a "Wine & Flowers Spring Celebration" and end in November with a two-weekend "Holiday Festival" drawing visitors from all over the country to the area. Other festivities include; "The Keuka Lake Barrel Tasting" in May, "Herbs & Wine Weekend" in June, "Cheese & Wine Festival" in July and the popular "Harvest Festival" the weekend after Labor Day.

As if those activities are not enough to keep a body busy, Judy also runs the tasting room which features gift and craft items from local artists. Fortunately for the Wiltbergers, they have four children who help out in the vineyard, winery and tasting room. "With a small business, you really count on your family to make it go," says Judy.

Keuka Spring Vineyards produces only about 2-3,000 gallons of wine each year, but they want to stay with limited production so they can concentrate on the wine's quality. They offer nine varieties of wine including, Chardonnay, Riesling, Seyval, Vignoles, Pinot Noir and four popular blended wines called "Crooked Lake White & Red" and "Harvest White & Blush." The proprietary wines are a blend of vinifera and hybrid grapes.

Each year the Wiltbergers purchase grapes from a neighbor to develop a winery "signature wine." Last year Len made a Merlot/Cabernet Sauvignon blend that was supposed to give them enough inventory for two years...it sold out in one summer. It's tough to keep good wine a secret in the Finger Lakes, that's why Keuka Spring Vineyards sells most everything they make each year, right out of their tasting room on Route 54.

King Ferry Winery

(dba Treleaven Wines)

LOCATION:	658 Lake Road
	King Ferry, NY 13081
	(315) 364-5100
HOURS:	10 AM to 5 PM, Mon.-Sat.
	Noon to 5 PM, Sunday
	Weekends only, Feb.-April
AMENITIES:	Tasting room, tours & gifts,
	Picnic area

What does a chatty cockatoo and a sandbox of kids have in common? The answer: They both have a beautiful view of Cayuga Lake from *outside* the King Ferry Winery.

King Ferry is the only winery on the east shore, not by design, but because most of the land on that side of the lake has been family-owned and used for dairy cattle for generations. There are rumors that some of that pastureland will be converted to vineyard, but to date only King Ferry has the pleasure of growing Chardonnay, Gewürztraminer, Riesling and Pinot Noir in this prime location.

Oliver, the talkative cockatoo, is an immediate hit with visitors and he loves the attention. As one employee said, "God forbid, you don't pay any attention to him, he'll make a heck of a racket." Children are not only fascinated by Oliver, but they also enjoy the sandbox toys while their parents visit the King Ferry tasting room. Later in the afternoon the family can get together at a picnic table and enjoy a beautiful sunset.

The origin of King Ferry Winery, according to employees, is that the owners Peter and Tacie Saltonstall were enjoying a bottle of wine with friends when one of the Saltonstalls remarked that "the wine was good, but we could make better." Someone threw down the gauntlet, the Saltonstalls picked it up, went to France to study winemaking for a year and, in 1984 planted the first of 17 acres of vines. I don't know the story on Oliver, he was creating a little scene at the time and I couldn't make out the rest of our conversation.

The folks at King Ferry Winery subscribe to the philosophy that "wine is a food, made to complement other food." On four "Open House" weekends in May, June, October and December, a mini Wine Fest is well-attended and well-stocked with good food, wine and neighborly companionship along with a lot of cockatoo kibitzing.

Knapp Vineyards Winery & Restaurant

LOCATION: 2770 County Road 128
Romulus, NY 14541
(607) 869-9271

HOURS: 10 AM to 5 PM, Mon.-Sat.
Noon to 5 PM, Sunday
Restaurant Open: May - Oct.
Lunch Mon.-Sat., Dinner Thurs.-Sat.
April, Nov. & Dec.
Lunch & Dinner, Thurs.-Sat.

AMENITIES: Tastings & tours, Retail gift shop,
Full service restaurant

The most complete family winery concept in the Finger Lakes is found at Knapp Vineyards, Winery and Restaurant. From a Culinary Institute of America trained chef, to two winemakers, there is a Knapp family member to oversee operations. From winemaker's weekends and barrel tasting parties, to intimate fine dining from the their lovely restaurant, again there is a Knapp family member to cater to your individual requirements.

Doug and Suzie Knapp have been grape-growers and wine producers for nearly 25 years. Their adventure in winemaking began with the purchase in 1971 of an old 100-acre chicken farm. The Knapp's have since planted grapes, started a winery, opened a sales and tasting facility, and in 1992 built a superb, full-service restaurant.

Son Jeffery Adema and his wife Louise manage the kitchen and dining room of the impressive Knapp Winery restaurant. Chef Jeffery creates an ever-changing menu to complement the Knapp wines. Combined with a vineyard view, the comfort of a winery garden and outstanding cuisine, the Knapp Restaurant is a popular attraction on the Cayuga Lake Wine Trail.

Lori Knapp has recently joined her father in sharing winemaking duties to form an unusual father/daughter winemaking team. The Knapps specialize in Chardonnay, Riesling, Seyval and Vignoles for their white wines and Pinot Noir, Cabernet Sauvignon and Cabernet Franc for the reds. A small production of *methode champenoise* champagne is also produced on the premises. Knapp wines have consistently won honors in national and international competitions as well as garnering deserved praise in the visitors' tasting room.

LAKESHORE

1991
CABERNET SAUVIGNON
Finger Lakes Table Wine

Contains Sulfites
Produced and Bottled by Lakeshore Winery Inc.
5132 Route 89, Romulus, NY 14541

Lakeshore Winery

LOCATION: 5132 Route 89
Romulus, NY 14541
(315) 549-7075

HOURS: 11 AM to 5 PM, Mon.-Sat.
Noon to 5 PM, Sunday
Closed Mon.-Thurs., Nov.-April

AMENITIES: Seminar tastings

Many wineries in the Finger Lakes region have a minimal tasting room charge that is refundable on purchases, but Lakeshore Winery not only gives complimentary tastings, they do so in a very unique fashion. Winemaker/owner John Bachman conducts a "wine seminar" complete with a sample compliment of food. "It sets us apart from everybody else," explains Bachman. "We spend time with our guests, get them to sit down, relax and have an enjoyable experience while we discuss wine and its marriage with food. It gets a little hectic on weekends, but the seminar format has become our trademark and people expect it."

Bachman takes his visitors on a tasting tour of Lakeshore wines in the comfortable farm setting of his hospitality room. The presentation lasts about twenty minutes, but sometimes during the week folks stick around to ask questions and further discuss wine. Its all very casual and extremely informative as Bachman tries to break down the mystique of wine with food. His philosophy and advice to customers is, "Don't worry about which wine goes with which food. Just find a wine you like, and enjoy it."

Lakeshore Winery's selection of wines include Chardonnay, Cabernet Sauvignon, Pinot Noir and Riesling. The Riesling is not molded in the usual semi-sweet fashion, but rather in a Germanic dry style that has been barrel-aged and complements light or spicy foods.

Lakeshore also offers two unusual red wines created from the French hybrid varieties Baco Noir and Maréchal Foch. The Baco Noir is fermented dry and produces an excellent full-bodied table wine. The Foch is used to create a mellow *nouveau* style wine in the fall of the harvest. Bright and fruity, the *nouveau* is a holiday hit at the winery. Catawba wines are still very popular in the Finger Lakes, so Lakeshore makes two wines of the native American variety, "Aunt Clara" and "Uncle Charlie," for the fun of it.

As you drive into the Lakeshore Winery parking lot and spot a crowd of people waiting to get in, don't be daunted. It's well worth the wait.

Lakewood Vineyards

LOCATION: 4024 State Route 14
Watkins Glen, NY 14891
(607) 535-9252

HOURS: 10 AM to 5:30 PM, Mon.- Sat.
Noon to 6 PM, Sunday
Fri.-Sun. only, Jan.-April

AMENITIES: Tasting & tours, Picnic & kids facilities,
Special winery events, Newsletter

Lakewood
Vineyards
1992
FINGER LAKES
Cayuga White
TABLE WINE

Most farm wineries are named after the families that started them. Some are named after the area or nearby landmarks. Still others received their names by a quirk of fate. When the Stamp family moved back to the Finger Lakes from Maryland in the 1950's, they dutifully reported their forwarding address as Lake Road, Watkins Glen, New York. As only the post office can do, the address was written on the records as *Lakeroad*. Then another postal clerk further complicated matters when forwarding mail came addressed as *Lakewood* (only the Post Office knows why). The name stuck and "the more we used Lakewood, the more we liked it," says family patriarch Monty Stamp. Hence the name Lakewood Farm. In 1989, Lakewood Vineyards became the name of the family farm winery.

The Lakewood Vineyards winery is a landmark in itself. It's difficult to miss the striking A-frame building and the rose bushes leading to the winery along Seneca Lake's Route 14. The rose has become the family's trademark over the years.

Lakewood makes a variety of wines using native American *Labrusca* grapes as well as hybrids and *Vinifera* varieties. Chardonnay, Pinot Noir and Niagara head the list of Lakewood wines as well as their popular "Long Stem White" and "Long Stem Red." Another wine that seems to sell very well is something called *Claciovinum* which is an "ice wine" made from the Delaware grape and only sells for about $9 - a very unusual combination.

The Stamp family does a good job marketing their products through their newsletter and tasting room and they also seem to have a good time doing it. The summer season is filled with winery events including "Do It Yourselfer" weekends where you can purchase a complete steak dinner for two for under $35. The catch is you have to cook it yourself. Don't worry, a bottle of Lakewood Vineyards wine comes with the package for moral support.

Lamoreaux Landing Wine Cellars

LOCATION: 9224 Route 414
Lodi, NY 14860
(607) 582-6011

HOURS: 10 AM to 5 PM, Mon.-Sat.
Noon to 5 PM, Sunday

AMENITIES: Tasting & tours
Picnic facilities

Lamoreaux Landing Wine Cellars is one of those phenomena that is "destined" for great things. That's extremely rare in the wine business, given the nature of the intense competition and the changing tastes of the consumer, but owner Mark Wagner seems to have his future under control. "I'm a grower, and four generations before me were growers," states Wagner. "My whole philosophy of winemaking comes from the vineyard. Wine is a natural product and we let it make itself. We just guide it along to produce good wines that go well with food."

Wagner attributes "superior soil content, gently sloping hills, unusual prevailing wind patterns, ample sunlight and proximity to the deep waters of Seneca Lake" as all individually important ingredients in the production of premium quality vinifera grapes and, therefore, first-class wines under the guidance of Wagner and his winemaker, Rob Thomas.

That may all be true, but Wagner is too modest about his winery's achievements. Since its beginning in 1992, Lamoreaux Landing, named for an old steamboat landing, has been "steam-rolling" the eastern wine world, winning top awards and medals for its wine in nearly every national and international competition it enters. Lamoreaux Landing's Sparkling Brut, Chardonnay, Dry and Semi-dry Riesling, and Pinot Noir are winning praise and turning heads from coast to coast.

You know there's something special about Lamoreaux Landing when you turn into the drive and are struck by the fantastic piece of architecture that majestically stands before you. You may wonder, "Is this a winery or an art gallery?" In actuality it is both. The winery building, designed by California architect Bruce Corson, is decidedly modern in a style the winery calls "neo-Greek Revival" and it often houses extensive art exhibits throughout the year. Fortunately guests don't have to buy a ticket to view the picturesque landscapes overlooking Seneca Lake. Enter and sample some liquid "artwork" that is destined to bring fame to this gallery winery.

Leidenfrost Vineyards

LOCATION: Route 414
Hector, NY 14841
(607) 546-6612

HOURS: Noon to 5 PM, daily except Tues.
Weekends only during off-season

AMENITIES: Tasting room

ESTATE BOTTLED

Leidenfrost Vineyards

1993

FINGER LAKES TABLE WINE
Merlot
Grown, Produced & Bottled by Leidenfrost Vineyards
Hector, NY 14841 Ph. (607) 546 6612/2800
CONTAINS SULFITES

One of the most unique winery tasting rooms I have ever entered is the 24' x 20' log cabin at Leidenfrost Vineyards. The Finger Lakes area is populated with many old barns and turn-of-the-century buildings, but none are as rustic as the "Indian Trading Post" atmosphere at Leidenfrost. Unfortunately, this wonderfully quaint tasting room may be short lived since expansion of a new visitor's center is scheduled to be finished in the near future.

John Leidenfrost is a former professor of art, a graphic designer and an artist who inherited the vineyards from his father. Although Leidenfrost was not enamored with the farm business while growing up, he did enjoy helping his father make the family's supply of wine each fall. In 1987 he began his new career, though he still considers it a form of art. "Especially the red wines," claims Leidenfrost, "It's a real challenge to grow premium red grape varieties and make a quality red wine. I took on the tough ones first. If I could make a good Merlot or Pinot Noir, than I could make anything."

Leidenfrost believes the Seneca Lake area is ideally suited for red grape varieties, "We have a longer growing season here on the lake and it protects the hillside vineyards from severe cold." Leidenfrost has developed his own root stocks in order to personally plant his vineyards with Chardonnay, Riesling, Cabernet Sauvignon and others. "I'm amazed at how things have developed in such a short time," he says. "I grew up on a grape-growing farm, but I have had no formal training in winemaking except helping my father and reading books. I have done a lot by trial and error."

It's obvious that John Leidenfrost has learned well from his personal research and he has followed a successful philosophy of "starting by growing good quality fruit, then let the wine make itself and try not to spoil it with a lot of manipulation and chemical adulteration." He's succeeded with his wine, but we're going to miss that old log cabin tasting room.

Lucas Vineyards

LOCATION: 3862 County Road 150
Interlaken, NY 14847
(607) 532-4825

HOURS: 10:30 AM to 5:30 PM, Mon.-Sat.
Noon to 5:30 PM, Sunday
Weekends only, April, Nov. & Dec.
Closed Jan., Feb. & March

AMENITIES: Tastings & self-guided tours,
Picnic area, Light foods available

I am always intrigued when I see wine labels with such names as "Tug Boat White," "Evening Tide" and "Captain's Belle". There must be a story behind the names. At Lucas Vineyards you won't be disappointed because Bill Lucas is a genuine tug boat captain in New York harbors two weeks a month and a winery operator the rest of the time.

It sounds like a strange (and busy) life, but Lucas has the support and assistance of wife Ruth and two daughters, Ruthie and Stephanie. While Captain Bill is maneuvering ships in East Coast harbors, the Lucas ladies are managing the retail operation and hosting tour groups as winemaker Steve DiFrancesco tends to over 25,000 gallons of annual production.

Ruth and Bill Lucas grew up far from vineyards and the country life, they were both raised in the Bronx in New York City. As a young man Bill drove a Greyhound bus route through the Finger Lakes and decided that this is where he wanted to settle. In 1974, the Lucas' moved their young family to a small farm in the heart of the Finger Lakes.

Farm advisors told them they could make a good living growing grapes for area wineries. By 1980 they opened their own winery and begun winning a long list of medals and awards for Lucas wines.

Today, the stately home and winery is the center of visitor activity and special summer wine and food events. When you purchase a case of Lucas wine you automatically become a member of their Wine Club, complete with special discounts, and you are invited to the Annual Club Party (the highlight of the season).

Captain Bill would like to retire to the comforts of his country estate and just make wine, but recent additions and improvements have necessitated an additional couple of years of earning that "saltwater money" to pay the bills.

McGregor Vineyard and Winery

LOCATION: 5503 Dutch St.
(East side of Keuka Lake, off Rte. 54)
Dundee, NY 14837
(607) 292-3999

HOURS: 10 AM to 6 PM, Mon.-Sat.
11 AM to 6 PM, Sunday
11 AM to 4 PM, Jan. & Feb.

AMENITIES: Tasting room, Gift shop,
Picnic area, Special events

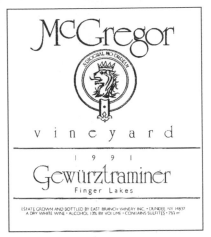

Beginning in 1971, when the McGregor family began planting premium *Vinifera* grapevines in an area highly dependent on native American grape varieties, the local residents knew there was something different about Bob McGregor. The problem was they couldn't decide if it was good or bad. Then he started planting Russian *Vinifera* varieties and eyes began to roll.

McGregor then opened a winery in 1980 and decided to take an alternate path in marketing his wine. He started a wine buying club he calls the "McGregor Winery Clan Club." Members pay an annual membership fee of $175 and receive a "Clan Pack" (usually limited edition wines) every two months plus special discounts and party privileges. After the membership began to swell, local skepticism turned to heightened interest as the McGregor tasting room facilities became increasingly active.

In 1988, Bob's wife, Marge, acknowledging the perfect combination of fresh strawberries and sparkling wine, came up with the idea of sponsoring the highly successful "Strawberries and Champagne" event each June. "What will these people think of next?" was the local query. Well, how about a "Spring Open House," or "Raspberries and Chocolate" in July, or how about creating a nouveau style wine so they can have an annual "Nouveau Party" in November? Will these people ever stop?

It doesn't look like anytime soon. Bob McGregor is continually looking for new ways to improve, expand and enhance his product line while Marge is pursuing the winery's interest in showcasing wine with food. And how fortunate for us!

The McGregor tasting room is a fun place to visit with its variety of unusual gift items, an excellent selection of well-made wines and a beautiful view of Keuka Lake. Picnic tables are available both outside and on the covered porch and the hospitality is plentiful.

Merritt Estate Winery

LOCATION: 2264 King Road
Forestville, NY 14062
(716) 965-4800

HOURS: 10 AM to 5 PM, Mon.-Sat.
1 PM to 5 PM, Sunday
Closed Jan.- March

AMENITIES: Tour, tasting & retail sales,
Pavilion picnic area

The Merritt Estate Winery is one of the many small family grape farms that took advantage of the New York Farm Winery Act of 1976. The state law allowed grape growers the opportunity to produce up to 50,000 gallons of wine per year and made grape growing and operating a small winery more economically feasible . Today, farm wineries are allowed to produce up to 150,000 gallons.

The Merritt Estate of 100 acres is planted primarily with the native American grape varieties Concord and Niagara, but Christi and William Merritt also produce some very good wines from the French hybrids Foch, DeChaunac and Seyval. They have also been developing some Chardonnay and Riesling vines to meet consumer demand.

Like most of the wineries in the Lake Erie region, Merritt is a small, hands-on family operation whose members enjoy what they are doing. That "enjoyment" may sometimes be challenged when Bill is trying to direct a busload of visitors around his tiny parking lot full of cars, but it is manifested during their "Anniversary September Fest" (the first weekend after Labor Day) when friends, customers and neighbors get together for a good time of food and wine and to celebrate the fall harvest.

The Merritt's are strong proponents of the natural marriage of wine with food. A complimentary recipe brochure of "Cooking with Merritt Wine" is available in the retail room and they invite customers to send in their favorite wine recipes to share, as well. The estate also has an open-air pavilion available for picnic lunches or for rental for large parties.

The Merritt Farm began as a modest grape producer for the giant Taylor Wine Company and intends to remain small, growing and producing premium wines primarily from their own vineyards. The Merritt's enjoy personally meeting and welcoming visitors to their cozy little country winery in the heart of New York State's largest grape-growing region.

New Land Vineyard

LOCATION: 577 Lerch Rd.
Geneva, NY 14456
(315) 585-4432

HOURS: Noon - 5 PM, Mon.-Thurs.
11 AM - 5 PM, Fri.-Sun.
April & Dec., weekends only
Closed Jan. - Mar.

AMENITIES: Tasting room, Picnic area

In the New Land Vineyard brochure is a quote from J.W. Mahoney that reads, "Whatever wine it may be, it is good; for, as the proverb says, 'In water you see your own face; in wine the heart of another'." From New Land wines you see not only the heart of another, but also the souls of a couple who have dedicated their energies to the propagation of quality wine.

Nancy and Andrew Burdick were two of the last pupils of the legendary Dr. Konstantin Frank and learned their trade with his guidance and the vigilant reading of books. Since 1986, they have perfected their skills the old-fashioned way, with steady hard work, study, trial and error.

The Burdicks hand-graft all their vines, manually plant and prune them, hand-pick the grapes and even cork and label each bottle of their highly sought-after premium wines...you guessed it... by hand. This is the true definition of "hand-crafted wine."

This husband and wife operation only produces 2-3,000 cases of wine each year on their 10-acre vineyard, even though they own an additional 30 acres that they rent out to a farmer. According to Nancy Burdick, "Our feeling is we would like to make better wine instead of more wine."

The Burdicks grow and produce only *vinifera* wine varieties including; Riesling, Chardonnay, Gewürztraminer, Sauvignon Blanc, Pinot Noir, Merlot and Cabernet Sauvignon. The emphasis at New Land is on red wines and they have incorporated the use of multiple clone selections (same grape variety with slight genetic differences) to give their wines more depth and character. They were using this method long before it became "in vogue" to use it in California.

The New Land Vineyard is small, a little out of the way and not very glitzy. It's a simple hard-working farm winery with a small tasting room in an open field overlooking a beautiful panoramic view of the vineyard and Seneca Lake. Don't miss the opportunity to experience some of the best wine in the region.

Olde Germania Wine Cellars

LOCATION: 8299 Pleasant Valley Road
Hammondsport, NY 14840
(607) 569-2218

HOURS: 10 AM to 5 PM, Mon.-Sat.
Noon to 5 PM, Sunday

AMENITIES: Tastings & tours,
Newsletter

Before Prohibition, Hammondsport, New York was the home of eight of the country's most prosperous wineries. Only three were to survive the devastation of thirteen "dry" years. One of the most renowned to fail was Germania Wine Cellars, whose wines dated back to 1861, the year that the first winery license was issued in the United States. By 1881 the winery had expanded to a capacity of 100,000 gallons, an enormous amount of wine in those days.

Eventually, the winery building was purchased and used by Great Western and then by Taylor Wine Company until it was closed in 1985. Today, that same building is being restored to its original design as a daily functioning winery under the watchful eye of President and winemaker, Jim Gifford.

Jim learned his trade in California (Fetzer and Domaine Mumm wineries) and in New York (Gold Seal and Glenora) before becoming a member of the start-up team at Olde Germania in 1994. Wines at Olde Germania Wine Cellars are made under two labels, Ste. Germaine (Brut Sparkling, Chardonnay and Pinot Noir) and Olde Germania (Red, White, Blush and Cream Sherry). According to Gifford, "Sparkling wines are my passion." It's safe to say that the old underground tunnels will soon be "bubbling" with sparkling wine bottles. "The Finger Lakes region is perfect for sparkling wine," claims Gifford, "It has the soil and climate much closer to France's Champagne region than any other location in the United States."

In addition, Gifford plans to expand the production of Solera Cream Sherry. "We inherited some old solera, so we're going to continue to add to it," says the enthusiastic winemaker. "Actually, we are going to have a broad spectrum of wines to offer people." An expanded Visitor's Center, picnic area and a redwood deck are also in the near future plans.

It looks as though the "new" Germania Wine Cellars is going to outlive all the other wine giants that have since become extinct in Hammondsport.

Poplar Ridge Vineyards

LOCATION: RD #1, Route 414
            Valois, NY 14888
            (607) 582-6421

HOURS: 10 AM to 5 PM, Mon.-Sat.
            Noon to 5 PM, Sunday
            Sat. & Sun. only, Nov. to May

AMENITIES: Tasting and retail room

Dave Bagley has been making wine in the Finger Lakes region for over twenty years so it was obvious that when he picked a spot for his own winery, it was going to be a good one. Bagley chose the sloping land on the east side of Seneca Lake. "The first part of this micro-climate is that we are in the lea of the Great Lakes which is good for considerable moderation of winter weather," explains Bagley. "With the winter's western or northwestern cold air having to cross two or more of the Great Lakes before it reaches here, that serves as a significant buffer. Now make that air come over Seneca Lake, which is 40 miles long, three miles across and whose surface temperature doesn't get colder than 42° F in an average year. Suddenly you have a lot of warm air pushing the westerlies up and over the hill behind our slope. The vines are rarely affected by severe winter weather. Even the cold winter of '94 when most areas were experiencing temperatures around -20° F, we never got below 9° F. In fact, it was the first time in 10 years that we went below zero."

This favorable micro-climate has allowed Bagley to grow Cabernet Sauvignon on his slopes for over 15 years. "It grows heartier than Riesling, which usually does well in cold weather regions, and Cabernet produces more consistently," claims Bagley, "but you need the right location and air drainage (movement of air currents through the vineyard rows) is crucial. The grapes won't do well on level ground, they must be on the slope."

Bagley uses the Cabernet and the Carmine grape, which is a cross between Merlot, Cabernet Sauvignon and Grenache, to make "Dave's Big Red." It's a sellout every year and has become somewhat of a trademark of "Big Dave Bagley." Dave is a "bear" of a man and some even say the big bear statue in front of his tasting room entrance may be a shirttail relative. I didn't ask.

Prejean Winery

LOCATION: 2634 Rt. 14
Penn Yan, NY 14527
(315) 536-7524

HOURS: 10 AM to 5 PM, Mon.-Sat.
Noon to 5 PM, Sunday
Closed Sundays, Jan. & Feb.

AMENITIES: Tasting room, Gift shop,
Picnic facilities,
Special winery events

Elizabeth and James Prejean moved to Seneca Lake from Louisiana to start a new career with James' retirement. In 1979, they planted their first grapevines and 1986 was the year of their first crush. It was at this point they decided to move forward with the winery. Unfortunately, James died in 1989 just as they began to get comfortable in their new life.

Elizabeth decided to carry on and enlisted the help of her son, Tom, to serve as winemaker and emotional support. Today, Elizabeth Prejean is known as New York State's only sole woman winery owner and a dedicated, capable person determined to succeed. She is active in a number of industry related groups and is president of the Seneca Lake Winery Association.

In memory of James, who was Cajun, Elizabeth created the "Prejean Cajun Club," which includes quarterly wine shipments of new releases and special products to members. It can get pretty cold in the Finger Lakes in February, but if you are a member of the Prejean Winery's Cajun Club you'll be plenty warm at the winery's annual Mardi Gras celebration. Along with the Mardi Gras event, complete with costumes, the Annual Cajun Fest in August is one of the area's biggest attractions.

When visitors are not frolicking to the music of a Dixieland Band during one of the Cajun celebrations, they are in the Prejean tasting room anxious for the opportunity to sample award-winning, estate-grown premium wines such as Merlot, Chardonnay, Johannisberg Riesling, Gewürztraminer, Foch, Cayuga and Vignoles. It's a warm and hospitable staff in the Prejean tasting room, willing and able to serve you a sample or two of some of the Finger Lakes' best. They'll also help you pick out a special gift from their large selection of unusual wine-related items.

For an opportunity to "Let the good times roll!" and to enjoy some fine premium Finger Lakes wine, be sure to look up Elizabeth Prejean at her Prejean "Cajun Club" Winery.

Roberian Vineyards

LOCATION: 2614 King Road
Sheridan, NY 14062
(716) 679-1620

HOURS: Noon to 6 PM, daily, April-Nov.

AMENITIES: Tasting & tours

Roberian

1992
VIDAL BLANC
New York State Semi-Dry White Wine

PRODUCED & BOTTLED BY ROBERIAN VINEYARDS, LTD
KING ROAD, SHERIDAN, NEW YORK
CONTAINS SULFITES   TABLE WINE

Right on the main route (Rte. 20) through the Lake Erie District is the little boutique winery of the not-so-little Roach family. This seventeen-member clan has ties back to 19th century grape farming in New York with six generations having toiled in the fields that now surround the roadside Roberian winery building.

Bob and Mary Ann Roach can usually be found around the tasting room greeting visitors while eldest son, David, is busy between his responsibilities as family winemaker and his "real" profession as a lawyer. Roberian is a blend of the names' of David's two oldest sons, *Rober*t and Bri*an*. All of the Roach's children, sons-in-law, daughters-in-law and grandchildren have labored in the fields or contributed in other ways at one time or another to establish the family winery.

While the Roach farm had been in the family for over 100 years, it laid dormant for a number of years while Bob pursued his career as an engineer in the aerospace industry. Now retired, he has his hands full trying to keep the struggling little winery in the black. "Between insurance premiums and government taxes, it gets pretty difficult. But, we have some ideas and high hopes that we'll keep it going in the family," says Roach.

Over the last century the family determined the best crops for its gravely land were grapes and tomatoes. Around the turn of the century the land was planted with Native American Concord for the "high flying" juice companies of the era. Today, influenced by the wines of Dr. Konstantin Frank, New York's famous proponent of the *Vinifera* grape, the Roach's have five acres planted with Chardonnay, Gewürztraminer and Cabernet Franc. They also harvest two acres of Vidal that they use in their popular "Bobwhite" blended wine.

Roberian Vineyards is a small family farm winery striving to maintain a proud tradition of agriculture on their land. It's not always easy, but they are determined to succeed for future generations.

Schloss Doepken Winery

LOCATION: East Main Road (Route 2)
Ripley, NY 14775
(716) 326-3636

HOURS: Noon to 5 PM, Daily

AMENITIES: Tasting room & gifts

Schloss, in German, means "castle" or "house." Doepken is the maiden name of Roxann Watso, wife and partner of winemaker/retired scientist John Simon Watso. Their tasting room is located in an old centennial farmhouse that has been converted into a provisional reception center. Nothing fancy, just good wine with opera music in the background.

On a busy weekend you'll have to exercise some patience while making your way to the small tasting table in the original dining room of the farmhouse. Take the time to wander around and examine the interesting wine-accessory gifts and packaged food products. Everything from grapeseed oil to pasta sauces is on display in the former living room. Once you reach the tasting area, you will most likely have the opportunity to meet winemaker Watso, taste a couple of his award-winning wines and discuss the finer points of growing grapes in this part of the country.

The small farm winery produces less than 6,000 gallons of wine, about one-third is devoted to Chardonnay and Riesling. French-American hybrid and native American vines are also grown in the gravelly soil on the premises. The soil here is part of a narrow band of elevated land from the Allegheny Plateau that runs parallel to Lake Erie and traps the moderating effects of the lake. The soil and the lake effect are the prominent elements that produce the superb grape-growing conditions in the area.

The property behind the farmhouse sits on an escarpment and offers a beautiful view overlooking Lake Erie. It is here that Watso would eventually like to build his real "Schloss," but things come slowly on the farm and growth is not easy in the wine business.

Schloss Doepkin is located on the far southwest end of Route 20. The highly visible grape-cluster highway signs make it very easy to visit the New York Lake Erie Region wineries on a single day-trip through this historic grape belt, the largest such area east of California.

Signore Winery

LOCATION: 153 White Church Rd.
            Brooktondale, NY 14817
            (607) 539-7935

HOURS: Noon to 5 PM, Sat. & Sun.
            April to December
            Weekdays by appointment

AMENITIES: Tastings & Italian garden

Hidden away in the most southern end of Cayuga Lake, where corn grows better than grapes, lies a very small (under 1,000 gallons) winery run by a charming retired couple who spend as much time in their Italian-style garden as they do in their winery. The Signore Winery is off the beaten wine trail because there are no sloping vineyards overlooking beautiful lakes, no fancy retail shops or giant storage tanks.

According to Dan and Ann Signore, whose home and converted garage/ winery is actually surrounded by cornfields, the climate is not conducive to grape-growing, so Signore Winery purchases its grapes and juice from growers on Cayuga and Seneca Lakes and then transforms the fruit to the style that is uniquely Signore.

Dan Signore is retired from the Engineering and Architecture Department at Cornell University located just up the road in Ithaca. After leaving the University in 1990, Signore took his home winemaking hobby one step further by going commercial. He produces wines of Chardonnay and Riesling, but his best efforts are shown in the French hybrid varieties of Baco Noir, Ravat, Foch and DeChaunac. As Ann Signore states, "Some people scoff at the idea of using the hybrids, but Dan blends in some Merlot or Cabernet Sauvignon with the red hybrids and ferments them dry. He creates a wonderful red table wine."

Ann Signore's pride and joy is the Italian garden next to the modest winery building. "We've done a lot of research in Italy to get an authentic look and feel," says Signore. "Everything is symmetrical and carefully matched with edgings and terra-cotta pots filled with various plants and flowers. We even have a fountain." During the summer, garden chairs and tables are placed in strategic spots so visitors can just sit, relax and take in the beauty.

If you are in the area of Ithaca, New York and Cornell University, take a few minutes to seek out the Signore Winery and have a glass of wine while enjoying the endeavors of the Signore's "works of nature."

Silver Thread Vineyard

LOCATION: 6075 Sirrine Road
(just off Route 414)
Trumansburg, NY 14886
(607) 387-9282

HOURS: Noon to 5 PM, Sat. & Sun.
Memorial Day weekend to Nov.

AMENITIES: Tastings & tours

The five acres of Silver Thread Vineyard were planted in 1982 on a gentle slope of Seneca Lake's east shore. Until 1991, the grapes were sold to neighboring wineries while the vines matured.   Only Chardonnay, Riesling and Pinot Noir grapes are raised in the vineyard, and all are organically grown. The folks of Silver Thread felt they should focus their efforts on the grape varieties that showed the best potential for Finger Lakes wine and to do so organically for the best wine quality.

Like all agriculture, mainstream grape-growing has become increasingly mechanized and dependent on agrochemical stimulants, with a goal for greater efficiency and higher yields. Silver Thread chose a different approach. Organic farming is labor intensive (pruning and harvesting is done by hand) and has a tendency to limit yields. The trade-off is that smaller crops tend to give more focused fruit flavors. Profitability, however, remains a major challenge.

The Silver Thread table wines are vinified dry and designed to blend with food and to develop with bottle aging. The wines are likened to lighter northern European wines in a style that complements lighter foods such as vegetable-oriented dishes, seafood, salads, pasta and poultry. The wine's natural acidity gives it structure for aging which brings out subtleties of flavor and aroma.

In a statement of environmental responsibility, Silver Thread Vineyard also prints its labels on recycled paper and uses corks that are not bleached with chlorine. There are no plastic or lead foil capsules covering the top of the bottles. Silver Thread folks feel the natural cork seal is all that's needed.

Taking the position of allowing the vines to produce naturally, with as little interference as possible, Silver Thread states, "Wine is the vineyard's memory of each growing season, which differs from every other. We try to celebrate those differences." The image of a turtle on their labels, which is an earth symbol in the culture of the local Iroquois people, is a constant reminder of their mission.

Six Mile Creek Vineyard

LOCATION: 1553 Slatervile Rd.
Ithaca, NY 14850
(607) 272-WINE

HOURS: Noon to 5:30 PM, Daily
Weekends only, Jan.- May

AMENITIES: Tastings and tours, Picnic Area

The Six Mile Creek Vineyard is the most southern vineyard site in the Cayuga Lake region with a magnificent view from its outside patio area where visitors enjoy a glass of wine in an informal and relaxing atmosphere.

Owners Roger and Nancy Battistella best describe their winery setting, "Nestled on the southwest slope of a lovely valley, the winery commands views of undulating meadows interspersed with stands of evergreens and hardwoods. A network of hiking and cross country ski trails skirt the rims of tranquil gorges, including overlooks of picturesque Six Mile Creek."

The Six Mile Creek brochure continues, "Situated on historic ground containing a pre-Civil War cemetery and stagecoach stop, the winery is in a restored turn-of-the-century Dutch-reform barn of post and beam construction. The barn is a well known area landmark."

Roger Battistella teaches at Cornell University in Ithaca and had been an amateur winemaker for over twenty years. In 1981, he planted his first vines and opened the winery with is wife in 1987. Together they have established a very pleasant and cordial winery attraction for visitors.

The wines of Six Mile Creek Vineyard are a combination of *vinifera* and hybrid grape varieties. Ranging from Chardonnay and Riesling to Seyval and Foch, the wines are very palatable and refreshing with plenty of lingering fruit flavors. Battistella is also fond of blending grape varieties to produce some proprietary styles that are unique to his winery. "Ithaca Red", a Chancellor/Foch blend, is an excellent companion for red sauce pasta or grilled meat. The "Pasa Tiempo" is a blend of Riesling and Seyval which creates a crisp finish and a good marriage with fish at the dinner table.

The area around Ithaca, New York is very charming and quaint. One easily senses the overtones of America's early history to the point of excitement for the dedicated disciple. Six Mile Creek Vineyard is very much a part of the area's history, yet its friendly hospitality and distinctive wines are very much today.

Squaw Point Winery
(a.k.a. "The Barrel People")

LOCATION: Poplar Road off Route 14
Dundee, NY 14837
(607) 243-8602

HOURS: 10 AM to 5 PM, Mon.-Sat.
Noon to 5 PM, Sunday
Closed Nov.- April

AMENITIES: Tastings, Retail gift center,
Picnic facilities

The wine trade is made up of many different personality types. Some strong while others are meek, some aggressive and still others are simply passive. Whatever the type they are easily identifiable, except for one couple.

David and Clorise Miles, proprietors of Squaw Point Winery (a.k.a. "The Barrel People") have an identity crisis. Their New York farm winery license identifies them as Squaw Point Winery, but customers and neighbors know them as "The Barrel People." It seems David Miles decided one day to build some people figurines out of old used barrels, tubing, hubcaps and other junk lying around. He decorated them and placed them along Route 14 as an attention-getter for passersby. One crazy idea lead to another and suddenly David had a whole community of "Barrel People" lining the road with curiosity seekers pulling into the winery of the "Barrel People" to check it out and sample the wine. Today, even the winery's labels are part Squaw Point Winery and some simply say, "The Barrel People."

To complicate matters even further, the Miles' have now adopted another mascot logo — a frog. "We like to do things the unusual way," says Clorise Miles. But they have fun doing it and the customers love the eccentricities of the winery and the uniqueness of the antiques and craft items in the retail gift shop.

The Miles' don't worry about Squaw Point Winery's (a.k.a. "The Barrel People") identity so they utilize all the varieties of grapes available in the region to produce an extensive selection of wine styles from dry to "exotic"... something for everybody. Squaw Point Winery also has a tasting room in Watkins Glen with everything you'd expect from folks that build barrel people, have frogs as mascots and make wines called, "Leon & Friends," "Moonglow," "Sweetheart" and "IRBY." The tasting room is also an arcade fun center. Go figure!

Standing Stone Vineyards

LOCATION: 9934 Route 414
           Valois, NY 14888
           (607) 582-6051

HOURS: 11 AM to 5 PM, Fri. & Sat.
           Noon to 5 PM, Sunday

AMENITIES: Tasting room

Early Dutch settlers came to the Finger Lakes region to trade with the Seneca Indians - the "People of the Standing Stone." They discovered a lake formed by Ice Age glaciers and surrounded by beautiful slopes and fertile land. The area later became part of the largest grape-producing region in the United States and the Finger Lakes retained that distinction for many years until the development of the grape industry in California.

The Macinski's came to Seneca Lake looking not for native cultures, but rather in pursuit of an interest that they could both enjoy together. Tom Macinski is a dentist and his wife, Martha, is a lawyer. They needed a weekend refuge from their day-to-day professional schedules, however, neither of them were "sit around and do nothing" people so they looked for a side business they could develop together.

Tom had been an amateur winemaker for a number of years and Martha enjoyed the fruits of his labor so they proceeded in that direction. Their quest brought them to Seneca Lake and the site of their new winery operation - Standing Stone Vineyards. According to Martha Macinski, "We started small and we plan to grow as we can handle it. Our first year in 1994 we produced 2,000 gallons and sold out of everything. In 1995, we'll start the season with 4,000 gallons."

The Macinski's work at the winery on weekends plus weeknights during the harvest season. "It's hard work," says Martha, "but we're having a blast!" The Standing Stone label is on four varieties of wine; Chardonnay, Riesling, Gewürztraminer and the French-American hybrid Vidal. The Vidal is offered in two versions, Dry and Semi-dry and is extremely well-crafted.

The initial success of Standing Stone wines may have been a bit more than the Macinski's bargained for, and only time will tell what the future holds for them. Who knows, maybe the world is in the process of losing a lawyer and a dentist, and gaining a premium wine family.

Swedish Hill
Vineyards & Winery

LOCATION: 4565 Route 414
            Romulus, NY 14541
            (315) 549-8326
HOURS: 9 AM to 6 PM, Daily, year round
AMENITIES: Tastings & tours, Horse-drawn
            wagon vineyard tours,
            Gift shop, Picnic area,
            Calendar of special events

Swedish Hill Vineyards were first planted in 1969 with an assortment of native American, French hybrid and classic European grape varieties. Awaiting their time after the 1976 New York Farm Winery Act, Richard and Cynthia Peterson did not open their winery until 1986. Since then, the Petersons have built the second largest farm winery in the state with production reaching over 50,000 gallons per year.

The Petersons are not about to rest on the laurels of Swedish Hill's success. They are moving forward with two major projects. One is to improve their current products by experimenting with non-cork bottle closures to protect the wine. The wine industry is concerned with increased instances of poor quality corks allowing wine to pick up "off" aromas and tastes. Swedish Hill is willing to take a venturesome leadership role in solving the problem with synthetic and screwcap closures on some of their products.

The Peterson's second undertaking is the formation of a distillery to produce fruit brandies. Both items are enjoying consumer success in the marketplace and Swedish Hill has already committed to much of the equipment and as of this writing is only waiting for the proper licenses to be approved.

A trip to the Swedish Hill Winery is an enjoyable experience. The scenic landscape is accented with beautiful farmland and entering the tasting room is worth the visit in itself. A spacious retail room is jam-packed with winery antiques and paraphernalia as well as wine-related gift items of every type. Gift baskets are a specialty of the winery and just about every size, shape and description of basket and wine "goodies" and "trinkets" are offered.

There is a special event every month at the winery, so you may want to call ahead to make plans. Even if you just casually stop in, put on your shopping shoes, then finish the afternoon on the deck with a glass of wine, some light food and a wonderful country view.

Thorpe Vineyard

Thorpe Vineyard

Trillium

New York State
East Bay, Wayne County

PRODUCED AND BOTTLED BY THORPE VINEYARD
8150 CHIMNEY HEIGHTS BLVD., WOLCOTT, NY 14590 • 315-594-2502
BW - NY - 758   TABLE WINE   CONTAINS SULFITES

LOCATION: 8150 Chimney Heights Blvd.
             Wolcott, NY 14590
             (315) 594-2502

HOURS: Noon to 6 PM, Weekends
             Memorial Day thru Dec.

AMENITIES: Tastings, Picnic area

Thorpe Vineyard is not only one of the smallest wineries in the U.S., it's also one of the most isolated. Located right on the southern shore of Lake Ontario between Sodus and East Bay, Thorpe Vineyard is not part of any designated viticultural area, nor are there any winery neighbors for miles. The area is primarily apple country with orchards dominating the landscape of Upper New York's Wayne County.

Fumie Thorpe is the chief winemaker and bottle washer at Thorpe Vineyards. "I do everything here," she exclaims, "I only produce about 1,500 gallons, so I can handle it." Tending her four acres of vineyards, which Thorpe says has "a little of everything," and running the recently opened retail room keeps her busy. Her husband, who is in the construction business, helps out in the vineyards on occasion, but for the most part Thorpe Vineyard is a "one woman operation."

The Thorpes purchased the winery and vineyards in 1988 and Fumie learned the art of winemaking with on-the-job training. "I had help from the previous owner who learned winemaking from Dr. Konstantin Frank," explains Thorpe, "From that point, I learned as I went along." She has developed a mixture of wine offerings from classic European varietals like Chardonnay and Pinot Noir, to estate wines Thorpe calls "foxy blends," referring to the predominantly grapey fruit flavors of native American grapes. She also intends to tap into the readily accessible apple market with an apple wine. "We've had a lot of people ask why we don't make a wine from the local apples. So now we will," says Thorpe.

Thorpe Vineyard overlooks the shores of Lake Ontario and is located about 1/2 mile from Chimney Bluffs State Park. On a nice sunny weekend, the trip to the winery is a pleasant and scenic drive in the country. Pack a picnic basket and make a day of it at the beach and at the winery. What better combination?

Vetter Vineyards

LOCATION: East Main Road
Westfield, NY 14787
(716) 326-3100

HOURS: 10 AM to 5 PM, Mon.-Sat.
Noon to 5 PM, Sunday
Limited hours during winter

AMENITIES: Tasting room

Over half of New York's total vineyard acreage is in the Lake Erie Region. While the vast majority of the grapes are still juice Concords, some vineyards are planted with varieties used specifically for winemaking. An increasing number of *vinifera* plantings, primarily Chardonnay and Riesling are continually appearing in the vineyards.

Craig Vetter is one of those individuals who is propagating the use of French-American and classic European grape varieties. Chardonnay, Cabernet, Rielsing and Gewürztraminer dominate his 22 acres of hillside vineyards along with Seyval Blanc. The Vetter family planted their first premium vines in 1970 on a north-facing site that was originally planted with grapes in 1864.

The Vetter Winery on Route 20 looks like a converted retail storefront with large windows at the front of the tasting room. Inside there is not the usual romantic feel of an old barn winery so familiar in the area. The decor is stark, clean and functional, almost continental, with high ceilings, light walls and a well-lighted room. A cordial employee greets you from behind an unadorned tasting counter and invites you to sample some of the excellent wines that are available.

During the summer months, tours of the winery, located in the back of the building, are conducted for visitors. There are no caves or dingy wine cellars, just clean, state-of-the-art equipment used to make premium wines. Then it's back to the retail room where you can explore the shelves for your favorite wine or an assortment of wine-related gifts and a unique selection of wine jellies.

Your initial reaction to entering the Vetter tasting room may be more businesslike than fanciful, and you would be correct. The winery, the wines and the tasting room are contemporary and designed to reflect the modern technology that is being used at the Vetter Winery. The wines are clean and sophisticated, designed for enjoyable and responsible consumption.

Wagner Vineyards

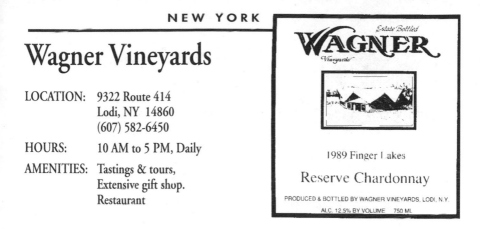

LOCATION: 9322 Route 414
Lodi, NY 14860
(607) 582-6450

HOURS: 10 AM to 5 PM, Daily

AMENITIES: Tastings & tours,
Extensive gift shop.
Restaurant

1989 Finger Lakes

Reserve Chardonnay

PRODUCED & BOTTLED BY WAGNER VINEYARDS, LODI, N.Y.
ALC. 12.5% BY VOLUME   750 ML.

As a lifelong resident and a grape-grower for over forty years, Bill Wagner is considered a modern-era pioneer and visionary for the Finger Lakes farm wineries. Bill began building his famous, self-designed octagon-shaped winery in 1975, even before the passage of the 1976 Farm Winery Act. "It seemed to be a foregone conclusion," states Wagner, "the farmers needed the help, the Governor and both political parties were supporting it, so I wanted to get going and be ready to start when the bill passed."

Ever since then, Bill Wagner has continually led the way to an onrush of new wineries which has consequently led to a steady stream of tourists in the Finger Lakes region. Most recently Wagner has taken on another project with the expansion of his Ginny Lee Cafe next door. What started out as a tent-covered deck serving sandwiches is now a full-fledged restaurant tending to guests for lunch or brunch indoors or *al fresco* on the deck overlooking a beautiful view of Seneca Lake. The Ginny Lee has also become the most desirable spot for a romantic bride's wedding reception.

Wagner Vineyards offers over 30 grape products including just about every grape variety found in the area. Many are award winners with the Wagner Ice Wines consistently receiving recognition every year. The winery's success can be attributed to an emphasis on quality control. From soil to wine, each step of the viticultural and winemaking process is subject to strict standards of excellence. All Wagner wines are 100% estate grown on over 100 acres of vineyards under the direct supervision of Bill Wagner. When he's not in the fields tending his crop, or in the winery sampling the progress of another award-winning wine, Bill may be found wandering the tasting room, gift shop or cafe making sure all his guests are being cared for.

As Bill Wagner is fond of saying, "This business is extremely challenging, to say the least." Yes, Bill, and nobody does it better!

Widmer Wine Cellars
(Canandaigua Wine Company)

LOCATION: 1 Lake Niagara Lane
Naples, NY 14512
(716) 394-6311

HOURS: 10 AM to 4 PM, Mon.- Sat.
Noon to 4:30 PM, Sunday

AMENITIES: Tastings & tours, Gift shop,
Picnic facilities

Around the turn of the 20th century, John Jacob Widmer played a pivotal role in the development of the grape industry in New York State. Widmer built his wine trade in the Naples Valley which was at one time the southern end of Canandaigua Lake. The glacial soil conditions in this area are very porous and shaley, ideal for growing grape vines. Widmer's grape business prospered and others were encouraged to follow his example in developing the famous Finger Lakes grape industry.

Today, Widmer Wine Cellars is a subsidiary of the conglomerate Canandaigua Wine Company which also produces New York State wines under the Taylor, J. Rogét, Great Western and Manischewitz labels as well as a number of West Coast wines. The Canandaigua Wine Company is one of the largest wineries in North America, second only to the giant Gallo winery in California.

The "Grand Tour" at Widmer Wine Cellars is a complete winemaking experience. From the magnificent views of the Naples Valley, to a tour of the 100-year old winery and museum, it is an exciting journey through history. Once your tour enters the heart of the winery, however, you'll marvel at the state-of-the-art efficiency being utilized in this massive production facility.

The tour ends with a free tasting of Widmer's wines and champagne at the "Wine and Food Center." Here you can also wander through a myriad of gift suggestions from food and wine books and wine-related accessories, to gourmet foods and homemade jellies. You may even wish to purchase a couple of bottles of your favorite Widmer wine.

The Canandaigua Wine Company tasting room is located in the beautiful Sonnenberg Gardens at 151 Charlotte St. in the city of Canandaigua. The Gardens and the tasting room are open daily, but only from May to October. At Sonnenberg you will have the opportunity to sample any of the wines in the Canandaigua line.

Woodbury Vineyards

LOCATION: 3230 South Roberts Road
Dunkirk, NY 14048
(716) 679-9463

HOURS: 10 AM to 5 PM, Mon.-Sat.
Noon to 5 PM, Sunday
Closed major holidays

AMENITIES: Tours, tasting & gift shop,
Picnic area

"Woodbury Vineyards is a return to a different time, when quality was paramount and business more personal." So states a Woodbury brochure and it is exemplified in an attractive and busy tasting room at the winery. A well-trained staff takes visitors through a series of wine tastings and explains that Woodbury grows only the traditional European *vinifera* grape varieties of Chardonnay, Riesling, Cabernet Sauvignon and Gamay Beaujolais on its 100 acres near the eastern shore of Lake Erie. However, the winery also produces a dry white wine from the French hybrid grape variety called Seyval Blanc and plans on utilizing that variety as a base for its blended proprietary dry white wines.

Woodbury specializes in the production of Chardonnay and Riesling wines. The Riesling is being vinified in a refreshing semi-dry Germanic style. Additional wines from the winery, that frequently sell out soon after release, are the Woodbury *methode champenoise* sparkling wines including a Riesling sparkler with four years on the lees (the sediment byproduct of fermentation that adds complexity to the wine). A pleasant Blanc de Blancs also shows itself on occasion in the retail room before being promptly snapped up by admiring consumers.

The Woodbury family has cultivated the soil near Dunkirk since 1910. The grapes thrive in this glacier-formed area of gravel ridges. The deep, porous gravel soil rising from the lakeshore is highly permeable, allowing vine roots to reach down 20 to 30 feet. According to Gary Woodbury, "There is no soil like this anywhere else. With this kind of vine penetration, there is no need to irrigate, even in the hottest weather." As a result of this unique soil and the climatic warming effects of Lake Erie, the grape yields are consistently aromatic with excellent acid balance. From there on, it's up to the skill of the winemaker to craft the juice into award-winning wines. And Woodbury has done very nicely with over 70 medals from national and international competitions since 1980.

OHIO

(The Ohio wine industry consists of four wine regions in the state: Lake Erie, Ohio Heartland, Central Ohio and the Ohio River Valley. We will address only those wineries directly affected by the lake-effect micro-climates of the Great Lakes. In this case, it involves the wineries along the Lake Erie shoreline).

The story of this region's grape-growing is best told by the folks at the Ohio Wine Producers Association. "In the mid-nineteenth century, the south shore of Lake Erie was rapidly developing as a major population center. The immigrants of different ethnic groups arrived together but settled in local clusters, mostly determined by the availability of transportation and land for farming. Often they found dense forests and swampland, and converted it to vineyards because much of the soil in the region was too wet and heavy with clay for effective grain production."

"Certainly, the immigrants of the 1840's could not imagine the changes 150 years would bring, but they could still be proud that their values and pioneering attitudes were maintained by the generations which followed on the ground that they cleared. "

At one point, after the turn of the century, Ohio was recognized as the largest wine-producing state in the United States. The Lake Erie Bass Islands alone were once home to dozens of thriving wineries until the passage of the Prohibition Amendment in 1920. This had a devastating effect on many of the wineries, forcing them to close. Some survived by making "sacramental" wine or converting their vineyards to "juice" grapes. The *Labrusca* or native American grape varieties such as Catawba, Concord and Delaware are still a major part of the Ohio grape growing industry. The 1990's, however, are witnessing a budding of not only quality hybrid wines, but also European *vinifera* varieties such as Chardonnay, Riesling and Cabernet Sauvignon.

The turning point for the modern era in Ohio wine history came in the 1960's with the planting of French-American hybrid varieties in conjunction with a national "wine boom." Consequently, the wineries of Ohio display somewhat of a dual personality. Many of those along the Lake Erie tourist belt are little more than "micro-wineries" serving a refreshing "Pink Catawba" or "Sparkling Niagara" in a bar-like atmosphere. It's a good business and very popular among fun-loving vacationers, but one that will hardly bring recognition to the area as a premier wine producing region.

This same temperate-climate growing region is also home of the newly formed Lake Erie Quality Wine Alliance. Members of the Alliance represent a new generation of wine grower and winemaker who are introducing such classic grape varieties as Chardonnay, Pinot Noir and Pinot Gris in order to promote the region as a "cohesive viticultural area producing wines of distinction." Spanning 40,000 acres of vineyards in three states (Ohio, Pennsylvania and New York) the formation of this organization of wineries and growers should prove to be the beginning of an exciting new development in Great Lakes premium winemaking.

For more information on the wines and wineries of Ohio, contact:
The Ohio Wine Producers Association
822 North Tote Road
Austinburg, OH 44010
1-800-227-6972

Buccia Vineyards

LOCATION: 518 Gore Road
Conneaut, OH 44030
(216) 593-5976

HOURS: Open daily, Noon to 7 PM
Closed Sunday

AMENITIES: Tasting Room, Bed & Breakfast,
Gift shop, Picnic area

BUCCIA

Ashtabula County

Riesling

WHITE TABLEWINE

Produced and Bottled by
Buccia Vineyard Conneaut, Ohio
Alcohol 12% by Volume   Contains Sulfites

Sometimes visiting a winery is so much fun you don't want to leave. Fred and Joanna Buccia make it very difficult to leave their winery grounds by providing not only a rustic tasting room, a cordial staff and excellent wines, but also a romantic "getaway" bed & breakfast, complete with private hot tubs and the serenity of a country setting. The Buccia's recently added two more rooms to their present four-room operation and reservations are still three to four months in advance.

Fred Buccia had previously worked for AT&T and spent a number of years in local government service. As politics sometimes dictate, Buccia's boss was defeated in the fall of '94. "I've now decided to go at this winery and bed & breakfast business full-time," says Buccia, "so we will be expanding both the vineyard plantings and the B&B, as time goes on."

Buccia grows only French-American hybrid grapes such as Seyval, Vignoles and Baco Noir, but he also buys Riesling, Gamay Beaujolais and Chardonnay grapes from Lake Erie growers to round out his roster of wines. He sees a future in expanding his vineyards of Vignoles grapes because of its versatility and production of high-quality white wines. Buccia offers a semi-dry Vignoles and on occasion a Late-Harvest version when the vintage allows.

The Buccia family describes a visit to the winery as a "memorable outing." They invite visitors to "bring your family and enjoy a picturesque scene, ranging from the blue skies and intriguing vineyards of luscious deep burgundy grapes to the golden glow of the white grapes. Prepare your palate with alluring cheeses and breads, sip fine wines, stroll the spacious grounds, or relax at one of many arbor-covered picnic tables. Children are welcomed at the winery and non-alcoholic beverages are available for them." Now, that's a difficult invitation to turn down!

The Buccia Vineyard is unique with a quaint craft and gift corner, colorful landscape, and of course fine tasting wines.

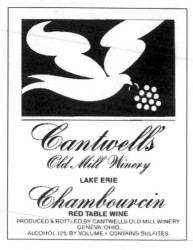

Cantwell's Old Mill Winery

LOCATION: 403 South Broadway
(Two miles North of I-90
on state route 534)
Geneva, OH 44041
(216) 466-5560

HOURS: 1 PM to 10 PM, Thursday
1 PM to 1 AM, Fri. & Sat.
1 PM to 8 PM, Sunday
Closed Thursday during winter

AMENITIES: Tasting bar & hospitality room,
Special events throughout the year,
Entertainment on Fri. & Sat.

Paul Cantwell is a trained metallurgist and computer specialist who retired from an Ohio steel company. A couple of decades ago the Cantwell's bought a home in Geneva, Ohio that was surrounded by fruit orchards. Cantwell decided to make use of the readily accessible resource and began tinkering with home-made wine. Eventually, Cantwell decided to expand his hobby into a commercial venture.

In 1986, Paul and Peggy Cantwell purchased the building that once housed an old grist mill. The mill, built in 1864, supplied the feed, grain and coal needs of Geneva area residents until well into the 1960's. Much of the original equipment still remains in the building. Today the rustic building is home for Cantwell's Old Mill Winery and the charm of a gone-by era is enhanced by hundreds of antiques and collectibles on display in the winery's hospitality rooms where tourists and locals gather to relax and enjoy themselves over a glass of wine.

The Old Mill Winery's list of wines include a range of dry full-bodied reds and soft whites, to heavy-bodied dessert style wines. Over 70% of sales are sweeter wines made from the native American *Labrusca* grapes. Concord, Niagara, Delaware and Catawba head the list. A pleasant, oaked Chardonnay and a dry Gewurztraminer are also available as well as an award-winning, semi-dry Vignoles and a *methodè champenoise* sparkling wine that has spent a minimum of 5 years on the yeast before being disgorged and bottled.

Large and small groups are welcome, and for special events the staff of the Old Mill Winery will reserve tables. To be notified of special events ask to be included on the Old Mill's mailing list.

Chalet Debonné Vineyards

LOCATION: 7734 Doty Road
Madison, OH 44057
(216) 466-3485

HOURS: Noon to 8 PM, Tues. - Sat.
Noon to 11 PM, Wed. & Fri.

AMENITIES: Tasting & hospitality room,
Gift shop, Weekend entertainment,
and special events

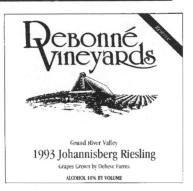

Grand River Valley
1993 Johannisberg Riesling
Grapes Grown by Debevc Farms
ALCOHOL 10% BY VOLUME

Chalet Debonné is one of Ohio's most "happening" wineries. Besides being an innovative leader in the production of fine quality wines from the Lake Erie Region, Chalet Debonné is a "hot spot" for fun and entertainment from May to September. What other winery do you know of that on any given weekend you may find an exhibition of model airplanes or antique steam engines, a Hot-Air Balloon Festival or kite flying, one of many diversified summer concerts, or a very unique "pet day" with judging of cutest to ugliest pet are among the variety of categories that can be entered? This kind of activity and excitement progresses to Labor Day weekend with a "Family Fun Day" with all sorts of games and activities for the entire family.

Chalet Debonné is more than just fun and games, however, it just happens to be part of the total concept of Debonné's energetic and marketing-savvy president, Tony Debevc. Tony is the grandson of Anton Debevc who founded the vineyards in 1916. Tony's father, Tony, Sr., tended the vineyards for almost 70 years and still caters to visitors in the tasting room.

When the grape business began to get sluggish in the late sixties, Tony, Sr. and Jr. established the winery as an outlet for their grapes. Since 1971, they have built one of the most successful winery operations in the state. Their best accomplishments, however, began in 1984 with the employment of their talented winemaker, Tony Carlucci. Carlucci has guided the winery to the establishment of a full line of products that now include nationally recognized premium Riesling and Chardonnay wines.

By visiting Chalet Debonné you will enjoy an informative and relaxed tour of the cellars.   Afterwards, you can sit down with a glass of wine and enjoy the rolling vineyards viewed from the glass-enclosed atrium room. You'll want to finish your stay by exploring the marvelous wine accessory and gift shop.

99

DLB Winery

DLB
Vineyards,
Inc.

Lake Erie **Cream Niagara**

Sweet Table Wine
Made & Bottled By • DLB Vineyards, Inc.
Westlake, Ohio 44145

LOCATION: 30311 Clemens Road
Westlake, OH 44145
(216) 899-1325

HOURS: 9 AM - 5 PM, Mon. - Fri.
9 AM - 1 PM, Sat.

AMENITIES: Tasting & tours, Retail sales,
Wine & beer making supplies

Don Bower is an enologist (one trained in the science of winemaking) with an academic degree in food chemistry. Since he grew up on a farm, the progression to grape-growing and winemaking was quite natural. Bower began his winemaking career in Michigan at what is now Warner Vineyards. After over ten years of working with native American grapes, French-American hybrids and European Vinifera varieties and producing many award-winning table wines, fruit-flavored grape wines, sherries and sparkling wines, Bower moved to Dover Vineyards in Ohio to continue his trade.

As a professional winemaker for over twenty-five years, Bower recognized an opportunity in the industry and turned his attention toward the growing amateur winemaker segment of the market. In 1989 he created DLB Vineyards, Inc. as a wholesale winemaking and beermaking supply company with a small retail store. DLB Vineyards sends beer and winemaking supplies all over the country to retail stores that supply home wine and beer hobbyists.

Being the incessant winemaker, however, Bower obtained a winery license in 1992 and created his own brand of wine. DLB Vineyards currently produces six varieties of wine from local grapes including: Pink Catawba, Cream Niagara, Vidal Blanc, Seyval Blanc, Chambourcin and a blended product of half Concord and half Niagara. In the fall, DLB Vineyards also offers fresh grape juice, advice, and supplies to home hobbyists. With nearly thirty years of experience working with Great Lakes fruit, Bower has become proficient in the use of the region's bountiful crops and his customers have come to rely on his invaluable advice and direction.

To visit DLB Vineyards' shop you must first find the Kasper Building on Clemens Road in Westlake, then proceed to the back of the building for the storefront entrance to the winery.

Dover Vineyards

LOCATION: 24945 Detroit Road
            Westlake, OH 44145
            (216) 871-0700

HOURS: Tues. 9:30 AM to 8 PM
            Wed.-Fri. 9:30 AM to 5 PM
            Sat. 9 AM to 4 PM
            Extended hours Sept. to Jan.

AMENITIES: Tasting room, Retail sales,
            Home winemaking & beer supplies,
            Tours by appointment

At one point in the 1980's, Dover Vineyards, a company originally founded in 1932 as a grape growers' co-op, was the second largest winery in Ohio behind the giant Meyer's Wine Company. In the latter part of the 80's, financial problems beset the company until A. D. McGlaughlin and Associates, Inc. purchased the winery out of receivership in 1992.

Today, the winery, retail store and the newly remodeled tasting room are located in a strip shopping center in Westlake and business has vastly improved, although Dover still only produces approximately one-tenth of the 100,000 case capacity of the winery. The retail storefront is adjacent to Lambert's Steak House & Tavern which is also a division of Dover Vineyards. The actual winery is located on two floors in the back portion of the building.

Dover Vineyards specializes in wines made from the three primary native American grape varieties grown in the area. Wines of Niagara, Catawba and Concord and a few fruit wines from peaches, blackberries and plums make up the complete repertoire of wine offerings from the company. Dover's *Half & Half* wine, which consists of a Concord and Niagara sweet blend, is the winery's popular trademark wine label distributed in retail stores throughout northern Ohio. "Cream Niagara" and "Pink Catawba" are two other sweet wines that follow the winery's original recipes. Each year the winemaker finds himself adjusting the wines to drier styles, however, as customer tastes change.

The Dover Vineyards' retail outlet is also a haven for amateur winemakers. During the juice-crushing season (September - December) the store is open extra hours to accommodate the multitude of customers seeking everything from fresh grape juice in bulk, to all types of winemaking supplies needed by home winemakers.

Ferrante Winery & Ristorante

LOCATION: 5585 State Route 307
Geneva, OH 44041
(216) 466-VINO

HOURS: Noon to 5 PM, Mon. & Tues.
Noon to 9 PM, Wed. & Thurs.
Noon to 11 PM, Fri. & Sat.
1 PM to 7 PM, Sunday
Open year round
Closed Mon. & Tues., Jan.-April

AMENITIES: Tasting bar, Winery tours,
On premises restaurant

Since 1937 the Ferrante family had transported the grapes from their vineyard in the Geneva area to their winery in Cleveland. Here they would make their wine and be close to their customers for easy distribution. In 1979, prompted by the growth of tourism along Interstate 90, the family built a spotless, modern facility at their vineyard location. The winery has grown to be one of the largest family-owned wineries in Ohio.

In 1989, the third generation of Ferrante children expanded the winery to include an Italian Ristorante. To the Ferrante's, and to most other Italian families, it is a natural progression to include food with wine. The restaurant is handsomely decorated, offers a scenic view of the sweeping vineyards, includes an open-air dining patio and provides a menu that is worth the trip by itself. If you would like to have your own private tasting of Ferrante wines, order one of the sampler selections with your meal.

Ferrante grows about twenty acres of native American grapes common in the Lake Erie Region like Niagara, Catawba and Concord. To meet the growing demand, however, winemaker Nicholas Ferrante purchases most of his grapes from quality growers along the entire Lake Erie Region from Ohio to New York. Ferrante makes a vast assortment of wines including French-American hybrids and European *vinifera* varieties.

You will find Ferrante wines well-balanced and flavorful, whatever your taste. The selection (more than 16 different styles from dry, complex, oak-aged Chardonnay to the fruity, medium sweet Bianco) will make an oenophile (wine-lover) out of everyone. The Ferrante Winery and Ristorante facility is a "must" stop as you visit the area. Call ahead to get the schedule of special events and activities sponsored by the winery.

Firelands Winery

LOCATION: 917 Bardshar Road
Sandusky, OH 44870
(419) 625-5474

HOURS: June - September
9 AM - 6 PM, Mon.-Sat.
1 PM - 5 PM, Sunday
October - May
9 AM - 5 PM, Mon.- Sat.

AMENITIES: Tasting room, Guided & self-guided, tours
Multi-media presentation, Extensive gift shop

Firelands Winery is named for the region in which it is located. A twenty-five mile long area along the southern shore of Lake Erie, between Toledo and Cleveland. The name Firelands originated during the Revolutionary War when British troops raided and burned coastal towns in Connecticut. The destruction and fire was so devastating that many families were left with nothing. In compensation for their losses, citizens were allotted land from Connecticut's Western Reserve in northern Ohio. This area became known as the Firelands.

Grape-growing began as early as 1836 by early immigrant settlers. German-born Edward Mantey was one of these settlers and he built a home and created a winery in 1880. The three generation history of the Mantey winery provides the background and basis for today's Firelands Wine Cooperative. The Cooperative serves as a central processing plant for four area wineries; Lonz, Mon Ami, Meyer's and Firelands.

The Firelands Winery is located right in the middle of the popular tourist area of Northern Ohio known as "Vacationland." A visit to the winery is a wonderful treat any time of the year. The retail shop is full of unusual and interesting gift ideas and the video is one of the best produced presentations on the area's colorful history and the magic of winemaking.

Firelands offers a wide range of wines from the area's traditional Catawbas and Concords to an award-winning *methode champenoise* sparkling wine made from Chardonnay and Pinot Noir grapes. In the past decade, new plantings of grape varieties such as Chardonnay, Pinot Noir, Cabernet Sauvignon and Riesling have begun to flourish in the vineyards right along side the prolific native American grapes. The Chardonnay table wine along with the sparkling wines have recently garnered some very distinguished awards and national recognition.

Grand River Wine Co.

vignoles
LAKE ERIE TABLEWINE

PRODUCED AND BOTTLED BY
GRAND RIVER WINE CO
MADISON, OHIO

Grand River Wine Company

LOCATION:	5750 South Madison Road
	Madison, Ohio 44057
	(216) 298-9838
HOURS:	1 PM - 8 PM, Mon., Wed. & Thurs.
	1 PM - 6 PM, Fri. & Sat.
AMENITIES:	Tasting room, Theater programs

Bill Worthy has successfully put together two loves of his life under one roof, theater and wine, and in that order. Worthy has a background as a banker, but there is no evidence of that life as the man sits in his favorite rocking chair with cap and cigar, taking life easy and not giving the worries of the world a second thought.

Worthy loves the theater and hosts the Mapleleaf Community Theater for a sixteen weekend season from April to November. The plays, which Worthy describes as "intellectually challenging theater," are all held outdoors on the winery's specially designed patio. Casting calls go out to actors from all over Northern Ohio and the Midwest and performances are warmly received by many regular customers of both the winery and the theater.

The Grand River Wine Company is a reflection of it's independent owner and is very low key and unpretentious. The walls of the small tasting room are monopolized by publicity pictures of actors who have performed at the winery.

The only price list is scribbled on a chalkboard at the end of the tasting bar. As Worthy explains, "we subscribe to real low key marketing. No hype. No 'puffery'. We don't enter wine competitions and we don't intend to grow much, by design." The Grand River Wine Company's production is "something under 10,000 gallons and we sell all we make," says Worthy.

What started as an extension of his hobby is now a cooperative effort between Worthy and his winemaker, Rik Kovacic. Their wines are well-made and diversified. Even a Grand River Sauvignon Blanc will show up on the chalkboard along side a Cayuga (Worthy doesn't like the name, so he calls his wine "Adrienne" after his daughter) or a hybrid grape variety such as Vignoles.

As Worthy so aptly puts it, "Grand River Wine Company is a good place to visit if you like, A...theater, and B...wine. Otherwise, you might just as well go on down the road."

104

Harpersfield Vineyards

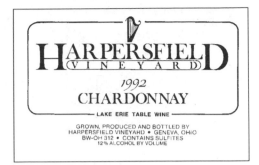

HARPERSFIELD VINEYARD
1992
CHARDONNAY
—— LAKE ERIE TABLE WINE ——
GROWN, PRODUCED AND BOTTLED BY
HARPERSFIELD VINEYARD • GENEVA, OHIO
BW-OH 312 • CONTAINS SULFITES
12% ALCOHOL BY VOLUME

LOCATION: 6387 Rt 307 West
Geneva, OH 44041
(216) 466-4739

HOURS: By appointment Only

There are no grand driveways, fabulous winery structures, not even a sign. The only thing you will find at 6387 Route 307 West is a 50-acre farm with a modest-looking home. It's just down the road from the impressive looking Ferrante Winery, but if you haven't called to make an appointment, your search for Harpersfield Vineyards may be fruitless.

Difficult as it may be to visit the small, family owned and operated winery, it may well be worth the effort to experience their wines. Wes Gerlosky started "by the seat of our pants" in the grape-growing business in 1979. Where most of Gerlosky's Ohio counterparts have built their wineries on the strength of the plentiful Catawba, Concord and Niagara native grape varieties and gradually expanded to French-American hybrids and then most recently to European varieties, Gerlosky started right out with Riesling, Chardonnay and Gewurztraminer.

Gerlosky experimented in the field, calculated the hazards of Great Lakes weather and tasted a number of wine samples from all over the world to evaluate and form his own style. In 1986 he bottled the first Harpersfield wine, a Chardonnay. As his style of wine has evolved, the Chardonnay is comparable to the French white burgundy and the Riesling is made in a classical, semi-dry Germanic style.

Today, Gerlosky specializes in only the *vinifera* white wines of Chardonnay, Riesling, Gewurztraminer and most recently Pinot Gris. It is the citrus and spice taste of Gewurztraminer, however, that Gerlosky feels is destined to become "one of the most highly regarded wines of the Lake Erie region."

All of the nearly 2,000 cases of Harpersfield wines are grown, produced and bottled on the premises, which by U.S. law makes them "Estate Bottled" wines, an inference of high quality. There are many Harpersfield Vineyard customers, however, who say that because of the hands-on operation of this small winery the wines, in fact, deserve the high quality reference. The Gerlosky's have a thought-provoking slogan that proclaims, "Harpersfield Vineyard Wines are nourishing...theological...and banish depression!" Amen, to that, brother!

Heineman Winery

LOCATION: Put-in-Bay, OH 43456
(419) 285-2811

HOURS: April - November 15
10 AM -10 PM, Mon.-Sat.
Noon - 7 PM, Sunday
Tours daily 11 AM - 5 PM, May-Oct.

AMENITIES: Tasting room & hospitality center,
Gift shop, Winery tour,
Celestite crystal cave tour

The Heineman Winery was founded in 1888 by Gustav Heineman, an immigrant from Baden-Baden, Germany, a world-renowned grape growing region. Heineman chose the Lake Erie island of Put-in-Bay to establish his winery because of its reputation for growing quality grapes as a result of ideal soil conditions and the long growing season tempered by Lake effect climate. These favorable conditions have allowed Heineman's to continue a tradition of winemaking on the island for four generations.

The Heineman Winery survived the devastating Prohibition era by selling unfermented grape juice. Today, Heineman's is the only winery left on the island that once was home to seventeen thriving wineries in 1900. The winery is now owned by the amiable Louie Heineman, grandson of the founder. Louie's son, Edward, is the current winemaker and according to his father, "he makes better wine than I ever did."

Heineman's uses primarily the native American grapes of Concord and Catawba to make their wine. Ives, Delaware, Niagara, Riesling, Vidal, Seyval and Chancellor are the other varieties grown on the neighboring North and South Bass islands for the wines of Heineman. Most recently, Edward, introduced a Chardonnay varietal wine that is fast becoming a hit with visitors to the tasting room.

Heineman's is one of the few wineries geared for the entire family. The newly expanded tasting room and the "wine garden" patio offer an extended selection of non-alcoholic juices. In addition, the winery conducts tours through the winery and Crystal Cave, a deposit of celestite crystals which form the world's largest geodes (geodes are normally small hollow rocks with crystal linings). The tours culminate with a complimentary glass of wine or grape juice.

Johlin Century Winery

LOCATION: 3935 Corduroy Road
Oregon, OH 43616
(419) 693-6288

HOURS: 11 AM to 6 PM
Monday - Saturday, Year round

AMENITIES: Tasting & sales room,
Country Arts & Crafts

The first Johlin came to Oregon, Ohio from Freiburgim-Breisgau on the fringe of Germany's Rhine River vineyard area in the mid-1860's. Richard Johlin is the third generation of the Johlin Family to work the land while his son tends the 160 acres of soy beans on the property. Richard purchases local grapes to produce about 5,000 gallons of wine each fall.

Johlin has a regular clientele that comes primarily from the Toledo area. "My customers are accustomed to the wines we've been making here for some time," states Johlin, "wines made from the traditional grapes of the region like Niagara and Catawba." Johlin has a very strong feeling about the trend toward the European grape varieties. "This region is just not right for them. Maybe some of the hybrids, but not the *vinifera* varieties. One of my neighbors complains that he has to replant every four or five years because of winter damage. They just don't work this far west. The winds off the lake are much colder here then they are east of Cleveland," he claims.

Whether he's right or wrong doesn't matter. "I'm 68 and it would be too much extra work to change now," says Johlin, "besides, my customers like the wines just the way they are." Johlin did add a little change when he recently introduced a Honey (Mead) wine, and occasionally he'll produce some fruit wines.

In 1989, Mrs. Johlin opened "Country Arts & Crafts" in the winery. The shop features many unique, one-of-a-kind, quality crafts by area artists and craftsman. If you're interested in country and Americana arts & crafts you'll find much to choose from in the shop, including a year-round Christmas Room with holiday decorations for home and tree.

The Johlin Century Winery is not open for winery tours, bus tours or special events. "That's too much extra work, too!" claims Johlin. However, stop in and taste the wine and browse to your heart's content in the enchanting Country Arts & Crafts shop and maybe you'll decide to take home a couple of bottles of Johlin wine.

John Christ Winery

American
JOHANNISBERG RIESLING
Wine
Contains Sulfites
Alcohol 12½% by Volume
Produced and Bottled by JOHN CHRIST WINERY, Avon Lake, Ohio
Bonded Winery No. 253
For Sale in Ohio Only

LOCATION: 32421 Walker Road
Avon Lake, OH 44012
(216) 933-9672

HOURS: 10 AM to 7 PM, Mon.- Thurs.
10 AM to Midnight, Fri. & Sat.

AMENITIES: Hospitality/Tasting Room,
Banquet Room facilities,
Private parties available on Sun.

After migrating from Macedonia, the late John Christ (pronounced *Chris-t*) and his wife Toda purchased a 23 acre vineyard/farm on the Lake Erie shore of Ohio. Two years later, in 1946, the John Christ Winery was established to supplement the family's income.

After World War II, John's son Alex assisted his father in the vineyard while working full-time at B.F. Goodrich down the road. In 1969, Alex assumed full-time winemaking responsibilities. Today, with the assistance of his son-in-law, Jeff Martin, Alex Christ has achieved recognition and success for the family winery.

The John Christ Winery grows primarily native American grape varieties such as Niagara and Concord, but purchases French hybrid and European *vinifera* varieties from their neighbors at Chalet Debonnè and Klingshirn Wineries. All of the John Christ wines are sold out of the retail room or consumed on the premises. A hospitality room was built on top of the original wine cellar to offer a cozy and unique gathering spot for guests and neighbors to get together and engage in conversation over a well-made glass of wine. According to Alex Christ, "Folks come in and create their own entertainment, we just supply the wine, some cheese and sausage, crackers and the atmosphere for a relaxing good time."

The room is decorated in a European motif complete with a tasting bar and a wood-burning stove to warm the winter days. During the summer, visitors can have a glass of wine from an extensive list out on the patio overlooking the vineyards. The setting is so enticing that the owners of the golf course adjoining the vineyard have approached the family about creating a total leisure-living environment with condominiums built around the golf course, the vineyard and the winery. This could prove to be an interesting development over the next few years. Until such time, the Christ family is still extending invitations to one and all to visit the winery and treat themselves to a glass of their wine in the delightful hospitality room.

Kelley's Island Wine Company

Indian Red
A crisp mellow Table Wine
Blended from European grape varieties

Bottled for
Kelley's Island Wine Co   Kelley's Island, OH 43438

LOCATION: Woodford Rd
(1/2 mile east of the water tower)
Kelleys Island, OH 43438

HOURS: June, July & August:
10 AM - 7 PM, Mon.- Sat.
Noon - 5 PM, Sunday
May, Sept. & Oct.:
Noon - 5 PM, Fri.- Sun.
Closed Nov. - April

AMENITIES: Tasting room, Wine garden, Gift shoppe

The glaciers which retreated from Northern Ohio at the end of the Ice Age some 10,000 years ago are credited with creating the micro-climates that are enjoyed today by the grape growers of the Lake Erie islands. The temperate effects of the lake create a long cool growing season, much like the classic wine districts of France and Germany. Early European settlers recognized the similarities and planted grapes to reproduce the nectar they remembered from their homeland.

The site of the Zettler Family Vineyard was first planted with grapes in 1854 and the original Kelley's Island Wine Company was one of the largest in the U.S. Prohibition destroyed the industry and the Kelley's Island Wine Company along with it.

In 1980, the Zettler family began replanting the vineyard site with both hybrid and *vinifera* grape varieties. The winery building was renovated from an old Civil War era stone farm house and the Kelley's Island Wine Company was back in business a year later.

Today, the Zettler Family Vineyard is one of a few Ohio vineyards to accept the challenge of growing the world's two most noble white wine grapes, the Chardonnay of France and the Riesling of Germany. Visitors have the opportunity to taste the results of the family's efforts in the tasting room or in the Country Wine Garden. The garden is an acre of open grass shaded by spreading sugar maples and surrounded by flowers, grapevines, and herbs. Picnic tables on the grass, a covered pavilion, light food and non-alcoholic beverages are also available at Kelley's Island Wine Co.

Before you depart on the ferry boat back to Sandusky, be sure to stop in the gift shoppe and check out the "Grape Gifts" selection of wine related items, souvenirs, tee-shirts and Nora's herbs and herbed wine vinegars.

Klingshirn Winery

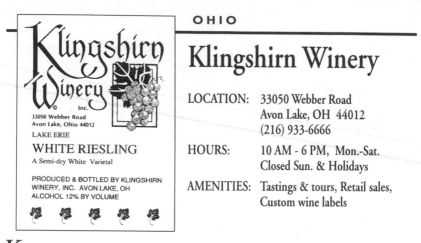

LOCATION: 33050 Webber Road
Avon Lake, OH 44012
(216) 933-6666

HOURS: 10 AM - 6 PM, Mon.-Sat.
Closed Sun. & Holidays

AMENITIES: Tastings & tours, Retail sales,
Custom wine labels

Klingshirn Winery is a third generation family farm winery. Albert Klingshirn developed a lucrative grape juice trade during Prohibition only to see it disintegrate after Repeal leaving him without a market for his fruit. With a large surplus of grapes, Klingshirn decided to produce wine commercially in his home. In 1935 he officially became a winery with twenty 50-gallon wooden barrels in the cellar. Since his first move seemed to effectively solve the problem of what to do with the grapes, Klingshirn then built an actual winery facility for two hundred barrels plus storage and a sales room.

Albert's son Allan came into the family wine business and expanded the winery as business dictated. By 1978, the original winery had increased four times and the 50-gallon barrels were replaced by large wooden casks and stainless steel tanks. Business was so good that Allan's youngest son, Lee, could go to college and get a degree in Viticulture and Enology. Lee is now the winemaker at Klingshirn Winery and works with his parents to continue the family tradition.

With only a small amount of part-time help, the winery manages 15 acres of grapes, bottling up to 10,000 gallons of wine annually. They feature sixteen different varieties of table wine and three types of sparkling wine. The Klingshirn wine list includes the region's traditional Concord, Catawba and Niagara offerings plus impressive samples of Riesling and Chardonnay. The Klingshirn champagnes include a native American grape blend, a French hybrid blend and an attractive sparkling Riesling.

Klingshirn's small size and personal attention to detail not only compliments the quality of the wine produced, but also puts them in a unique position to work with their customers as evidenced by their comprehensive "custom label" program for special occasions. Their selection of label graphics, imprinted with personal messages, is one of the best around.

Informal tours of the winery are available when time permits (not during the harvest season, however, unless you want to be put to work!)

Carl Limpert Winery

LOCATION: 28083 Detroit Road
           Westlake, OH 44145
HOURS: 8 AM to 10 PM, Mon.-Sat.
AMENITIES: Tasting & Retail Sales

AMERICAN
SWEET BURGUNDY
WINE
Produced and Bottled by
C.M. LIMPERT
28083 DETROIT ROAD
Westlake, Ohio
Phone: 871-0035
Alcohol 13% by Volume

There are many wineries in Ohio that have positioned their retail and tasting rooms in the high commerce areas of nearby towns to capture customers from the traffic that flows by. It is unusual, however, for a winery to have the total operation, including the vineyards, right in the midst of a growing community.

Carl Limpert started his winery in 1934 just after Prohibition when his fruit farm was still a long way from the center of town. Over the years the community grew and developed all around his modest four to five acres of land. Limpert continued growing grapes, peaches and plums and making wine. Urban growth didn't really affect him that much, he just tended to his vineyards and orchards and let things develop around him as they will.

Today, Carl Limpert is almost 90 years old, is confined to a wheelchair and requires constant care. He still sells wine off the back porch of his farm home right on main street. With the help of his assistants, Limpert still manages to produce a couple of thousand gallons of wine each year for his regular customers.

With the incapacitation of Limpert, the future of the winery seems uncertain. There are no heirs apparent to take over the winery operation and the orchards. Limpert's helpers maintain the vineyards of Niagara, Concord and Delaware and in the fall are directed by Limpert in the transformation of the grapes to his beloved wine. The wine is packaged only in three-liter jugs and secured with screw caps for ease of handling and efficiency of labor.

There are no winery tours (although visitors are welcome to walk around on their own, if they wish), fancy tasting rooms or slick multi-media presentations on the making of wine. Carl Limpert Winery is one of the state's smallest wineries that consists of a humble back porch tasting room, unpretentious wines and a simple farmer who has been doing something he loves for over sixty years.

Lonz Winery

LOCATION: Middle Bass Island
Middle Bass, OH 43446
(419) 285-5411

HOURS: Memorial Day to Labor Day
Noon to 7 PM, Sun. - Thurs.
Noon to 10 PM, Fri.
Noon to Midnight, Sat.
May and September
Slightly shorter hours

AMENITIES: Winery tours & slide presentation,
Gift shop & snack bar, Special events

The historic Lonz Winery is a literal "hot bed" of activity during the area's busy summer tourist season. The Bass Islands are in the heart of Ohio's vactionland, only a ferry boat ride away from the mainland and Cedar Point. The winery was first opened during the Civil War as the Golden Eagle Winery and by 1875 it was the largest wine producer in the United States. Today, you can take the family on a historic tour of the 100 year old wine cellars cut deep into the native limestone. The grapes, however, are crushed and the wines produced and bottled at the Firelands Wine Cooperative on the mainland.

Little did Peter Lonz realize in 1884 when he started producing wines on Middle Bass Island that his winery would become one of Ohio's premier tourist attractions. Aided by the construction of a magnificent Gothic winery building designed by George Lonz in 1934, tens of thousands of visitors have enjoyed a bottle of Lonz wine on the terrace overlooking the shimmering waters of Lake Erie dotted with boats of all sizes and types. Once summer kicks into full gear, the island "rocks" with a full schedule of live entertainment and special events. From sailboat racing and a 5K run, to a grape-stomping festival and barbeques, the action barely stops.

Due to its island location in Lake Erie it is only logical that the Lonz Winery take on a nautical theme. Their gift shoppe features nautical gifts of all types. Brass, ceramic and wood items are available as well as original works of art and a complete selection of wine accessories. Even the Lonz wine labels emphasize sailing ships and a "Captain's Table" line of wines.

Lonz is a perfect family venue with special family-oriented events on Wednesdays. Each day, playground and picnic facilities are available for everyone to enjoy. If you plan to visit the island winery, be sure to call ahead for the entertainment schedule and tour times.

Markko Vineyard

ADDRESS: R.D. 2, South Ridge Rd.
Conneaut, OH 44030
(216) 593-3197

HOURS: 11 AM to 6 PM, Mon. - Sat.
Closed Sunday
Calling ahead is recommended

AMENITIES: Tasting Room, Picnic Area

Since 1968

Markko

Conneaut Ohio

Chardonnay

Grown, Produced and Bottled By
Markko Vineyard, Conneaut, Ohio
Alcohol 11½% By Volume

Markko Vineyard is one of a long line of winery/vineyards that have been influenced by the famous Eastern U.S. pioneer winemaker and grower, Dr. Konstantin Frank. Dr. Frank told Arnulf "Arnie" Esterer and his partner, Tim Hubbard, that they could grow classic European *vinifera* grape varieties off the shores of Lake Erie and make excellent wine.

Esterer followed the advice of Dr. Frank and in 1968 the two partners began planting their 14 acres with Chardonnay, Riesling and Cabernet Sauvignon grapes. The land is devoted exclusively to the European grape varieties and the venture has proven successful. Some of the finest Chardonnay and Riesling wines of the Great Lakes region come from Markko Vineyard. Unfortunately, only a maximum of 3,000 cases are available in any one vintage. As Esterer puts it, "We're more of a demonstration winery in a lot of ways. We have to solve the problems and develop the winemaking technology for our area on a small scale. I just don't believe great wines can be made on a big scale. We don't want to get bigger, our job is to get better."

The extremely cold winter of 1994 was the most severe test for the cold sensitive grape varieties of Europe, but Markko Vineyard prevailed. "The winter of '94 presented an opportunity to learn, but it was not one we would hope to experience again," exclaims Esterer.

Visiting Markko Vineyard, and you must if you're in the area, is somewhat of an adventure. By following the Ohio Wine Producers Association's tour map down gravel roads to a driveway in the woods and a rustic winery building, you are first greeted by a friendly band of Markko "pups." The dogs are especially friendly and affectionate and seem to be the winery's mascots as well as the welcoming committee. Once inside the cabin-like tasting room a wonderful world of exquisite wines, along with their maker, is awaiting your pleasure.

MON AMI

AMERICAN

CHARDONNAY

VINTED & BOTTLED BY MON AMI WINE CO.
SANDUSKY, OHIO   ALC 11.5% BY VOL

Mon Ami Restaurant & Winery

LOCATION: 3845 East Wine Cellar Rd.
              (Just off Route 53, North of Route 2)
              Port Clinton, OH 43452
              (419) 797-4445
              (800) 777-4266

HOURS: Open daily, year round

AMENITIES: Restaurant, Sales & gift shop

Most winery/restaurant combinations develop their food service operation around the success of the winery trade. At Mon Ami, the emphasis is definitely on food. The winery is part of the Firelands Wine Cooperative which serves as the central processing plant for the 26 varieties of wine under the Mon Ami label. The restaurant is an extension of the Zappone family whose culinary history began with Grandma Zappone making pasta dishes above the family grocery store some 80 years ago.

More than 100 years ago, much of the countryside surrounding Mon Ami was devoted to the growing of Catawba grapes. Early immigrants found the limestone soil and the tempering effect of Lake Erie the perfect combination for growing grapes. The Mon Ami winery was constructed in 1872 of local native materials. Four to six foot thick limestone block walls, mortar from slated limestone, sand from the lakeshore and walnut from the surrounding woods were used in the construction of the winery building.

This building now houses the restaurant, sales and gift shop on the main floor, with banquet and private party facilities on the second floor, and a sparkling wine cellar in the basement just beneath the restaurant. The folks at Mon Ami like to point out that one of their award-winning wines, Delaware, is produced from "the gracefully sweet, Lake Erie Delaware grape." They make special note that "the grape is not named for the State of Delaware, U.S.A., but rather for the town of Delaware, Ohio where this native American grape was first cultivated." The Mon Ami people take great pride in their local history.

From May through September, the Mon Ami is one of the busiest places in the area. From "Jazz Outdoors" to live entertainment in the Chalet Lounge indoors, to various barbecues and an inviting dining room menu, the Mon Ami lives up to its cordial name; "My Friend." And, the Mon Ami is a great friend to have!

Northland Vineyard

LOCATION: 4018 Middle Ridge Rd
Perry, OH 44081
(216) 259-2652

HOURS: Noon to 6 PM, Tue.-Sat.
Closed Sunday & Monday

AMENITIES: Tasting room, Deck/picnic area

Some of the best career advice to give young people is "to find something you like to do, learn all you can about it and stick with it." While researching a senior class project, Richard Kovacic did just that. In fact, Bill Worthy of Grand River Wine Co. was so impressed with the young man's inquisitiveness and enthusiasm that he offered him a job at the winery. Fifteen years later, Kovacic is more knowledgeable, still young and still at Grand River, now as their highly qualified winemaker. He has also added ambition and dedication to his list of strong character traits.

In the spring of 1995, Richard Kovacic and his wife Catherine, opened their own small winery in addition to Richard's work at Grand River. The Northland Vineyard Winery is situated in a converted two-stalled garage next to the Kovacic family home near Route 20. Northland Vineyard is an extension of Richard's father's vineyards which used to consist of Concord grapes for juice and for the family roadside fruit-stand. "Gradually, housing projects replaced most of the vineyards, but we're going to replant the remaining fifteen acres," says Catherine Kovacic.

Northland Vineyards patterns itself after wineries the Kovacic's have visited in Canada on numerous occasions. "We really love the Ontario wine region and we like how easy it is to go from one winery to another while enjoying the area at the same time. We have a number of wineries near us and we'd like to encourage that same type of activity," explains Catherine, who presides over the business aspect of the couple's venture. She foresees adding an outside deck for visitors to enjoy a picnic and a glass of Northland wine as they tour the area wineries.

The Kovacic's are currently tending and developing three acres of their vineyard land and the vines are in their third and fourth leaf (growing season). "I'm really proud of what Richard has accomplished," Catherine says enthusiastically, "this is all he has ever done. It's his life. We're not a big farm, we're just simple people making wine." And doing a good job of it, too!

Old Firehouse Winery

LOCATION:	5499 Lake Rd., Box 310 Geneva-on-the-Lake, OH 44041 (216) 466-9300
HOURS:	Noon to 1 AM, daily Memorial Day to Labor Day, Weekends, Oct.-May
AMENITIES:	Tasting room, Full service restaurant, Outdoor facilities, Entertainment & special events, Bus and group tours welcome

A 1924 Dodge Firetruck, the city's original firebarn, a hospitality room full of nostalgic fire-fighting paraphernalia and the serene beauty of the Lake Erie shoreline are all features of this most unique winery. Located right in the heart of the resort town of Geneva-on-the-Lake, the Old Firehouse Winery sits on the Lake Erie shore and offers magnificent summer sunsets and fantastic winter landscapes. On weekends during the summer tourist season, however, "the joint starts jumpin!" From live entertainment, to an annual Celtic Fest, to clambakes and food extravaganzas, the fun doesn't stop at this popular gathering spot.

Don Woodward, one of the partners in the winery and a third generation volunteer firefighter, enjoys relaying the story of his unusual winery building. "After fruitlessly battling blazes with a 'bucket brigade', several local businessmen (one of which was Don's grandfather) chipped in and ordered a 1924 Graham Brothers firetruck. They now had a truck on the way, and had two immediate issues to address: a place to put the truck and who was going to be fire chief. Emery Tyler offered the use of his barn. Everyone was so grateful they promptly made him chief." Woodward continues, "In 1987, Dave Otto, his mom Joyce, and I looked at an old run-down barn and a rusting, 1924 firetruck, and decided we had our winery."

The Old Firehouse's wine list includes a variety of wine styles from dry to sweet, made primarily from Lake Erie region native American and French-American hybrid grapes. Only a small amount of Old Firehouse wine is actually produced on the premises (under 2,000 gallons), but they are nicely made, refreshing and add to the pleasure of a leisurely afternoon or casual evening on The Old Firehouse outdoor deck and gazebo.

Rolling Hills Winery

LOCATION: 768 S. Parrish Rd
           (1 1/2 miles west of Rt. 7)
           Conneaut, OH 44030
           (216) 599-8833

HOURS: 4-7 PM, Fridays
           Noon to 6 PM, Saturdays
           or by appointment

AMENITIES: Tasting room,
           Pavilion for picnic & catering,
           Bulk juices for home winemakers

Rolling Hills Winery

WHITE TABLE WINE
AUTUMN MIST
GROWN, PRODUCED AND BOTTLED BY
ROLLING HILLS WINERY
CONNEAUT, OHIO
ALCOHOL 10½ % BY VOLUME   CONTAINS SULFITES

Ray Palagyi's family property dates back to 1907 when the family was primarily in the cattle business. Today, his small Rolling Hills Winery is located in the same quiet country setting surrounded by eight acres of vineyards planted on rolling hills in Conneaut, Ohio wine country.

Palagyi grows and hand picks all his own fruit. "We buy nothing!" he emphasizes. The last few years he began experimenting with Zinfandel, Merlot and Cabernet Franc, "I was surprised they came through that hard winter of '94. We registered -23°F, but we had a good cover of snow to insulate the young vines." Palagyi expects to be able to make limited amounts of wine from these premium varieties within the next couple of years.

Also on the Rolling Hills wine list are two wines made from grapes not found anywhere else. "Autumn Mist" is made from an experimental white grape known only by its lab number, 10-63. There are only 150 vines of 10-63 in the world and they're all located in the vineyards of Rolling Hills. The grape makes a crisp, semi-dry white wine that Palagyi says, "Is hard to describe. The taste seems to vary each year depending on the growing conditions." The other obscure grape variety is named "Buffalo." A native American variety, from who knows where, it is a very dark red grape that Palagyi plans to "have fun with, as the vines mature."

Working with heavy equipment machinery at his "real" job during the week, Palagyi savors the delicate artistry of winemaking that developed from a hobby to a full blown weekend commitment in the basement of his home. "People kind of enjoy the homey atmosphere," says Palagyi, "and they'll bring their friends for a special party in our open-air pavilion. Everybody has a good time, good food and evidently they like my wine, too."

Steuk Wine Company

Lake Erie Black Pearl

a rich, dark, sweet, red wine

estate bottled   alcohol 10% by volume

produced and bottled by
steuk wine company sandusky, ohio 44870
contains sulfiting agents

LOCATION: 1001 Freemont Ave.
Sandusky, OH 44870
(419) 625-0803

HOURS: May - November
9 AM - 7:30 PM, Mon.-Sat.
10 AM - 6 PM, Sunday
December - April
9 AM - 6 PM, Mon.-Sat.
10 AM - 6 PM, Sunday

AMENITIES: Extensive farm market & gift shop,
Weekend events

The original Steuk Winery was founded in the 1850's. Five generations of Steuks cultivated the farm, vineyards and orchards. With the advent of Prohibition, the winery closed, and the family turned to the production of tree fruits and removed or abandoned much of the vineyard. In 1948 William K. Steuk, the fourth generation Steuk, reopened the winery and developed a little- known native American grape variety called "Black Pearl." To this day, wine made from Black Pearl grapes is only available at Steuk's.

Today, the family no longer operates the business but the Steuk name still identifies a busy country market at the intersection of Routes 2 and 6 on the west side of Sandusky. Tourists are constantly coming and going on their way to Cedar Point or the islands in Lake Erie just off the point. Families leave Steuk's with arms full of gourmet foods, hand-made gifts, fresh-pressed cider, wine and a variety of other unique gifts and collectibles to take back home. Local residents have also come to rely on Steuk's for plenty of weekend entertainment and special events as well.

Steuk's Country Market & Winery now features an on-premises bakery, kitchen, deli counter and, of course, the winery. The Steuk staff invites visitors to "relax on the 'Wine Deck' overlooking the orchard with a bottle of our fine wine and a delicious snack of cheese, fruit and home-made gourmet bread. Or put your feet up with a cup of gourmet coffee or tea and some fresh pastry!" Summertime favorites include cold cider and wines, and "old fashioned" lemonade. In the winter Steuk's warms you up with hot spiced cider or mulled wine along with one of their freshly baked pastries.

ONTARIO

The name Ontario is an old Iroquois word meaning "the shining waters." In the wine trade the name has come to mean "best kept secret." The Canadian province is surrounded by three of the Great Lakes: Lake Erie to the south, Lake Ontario to the northeast and Lake Huron to the northwest. All three shelter the land and, combined with the terrain, contribute to the successful growing of fruit.

There are three Designated Viticultural Areas (DVA) in Ontario: the Niagara Peninsula, which lies on the southwest shore of Lake Ontario; Pelee Island, located in Lake Erie; and Lake Erie North Shore, near Windsor. These areas produce 80% of the grapes used in Canadian wine production.

The climate within Niagara's vineyard country is the most significant of the three. Micro-climate zones exist throughout the area from the Niagara Escarpment, a ridge that was once the beach of an Ice Age lake, to the shores of Lake Ontario. The area to the south of the Niagara Escarpment rises some 200 feet, so that winter storms rolling in from the north and across Lake Ontario are raised and deflected. The best premium wines come from this region and the "Wine Route" signs make it easy to get around this scenic and historic area.

The Lake Erie North Shore has the most sunshine hours in Canada and as a result its fruit goes to market weeks before other parts of the province. However, the area also has higher humidity levels and temperatures are less stable creating the higher possibility of fungus problems. Windsor and Pelee Island are nearby which makes this area a very popular tourist center as well.

The Canadians have established a quality system similar to France's AOC and Italy's DOC called Vintners Quality Alliance (VQA). It not only sets the criteria for Ontario's quality wines, it also ensures that the wines live up to its specified standards. Before products can be marketed under the VQA medallion they must be tested and passed by a grading panel.

A specialty of the region is "Icewine" which rivals the world's best dessert wines. Ontario is fortunate to have the kind of winter climate that ensures Icewine can be made consistently year after year. Grapes are harvested naturally frozen on the vine at -7° C (20° F) or colder. It is while they are in this state of deep-freeze that they are pressed, extracting only the highly concentrated juice and leaving the water behind as ice. After vinting, this nectar results in a wine that is wonderfully sweet and fruitful. There is risk, however, particularly from birds and animals who like the concentrated sweet grapes, too. Consequently, during the fall months a visit to wine country is a weird experience with the sound of noisemakers and vineyards covered with netting. The hybrid Vidal and the classic Riesling make the best Icewine and because of the high labor intensity and low yields the price is expensive, ranging from $25 to $50 Canadian for a half (375ml) bottle.

Maps and informative brochures are available upon request from:
The Wine Council of Ontario
35 Maywood Ave.
St. Catharines, Ontario, Canada L2R 1C5
(905) 684-8070

Andres/Peller Estates

LOCATION: 697 South Service Road
            (at Kelson Avenue)
            Winona, Ontario L8E 5S4
            (905) 643-8687

HOURS: 10 AM to 5 PM, daily
            Tours at 1 PM & 3 PM

AMENITIES: Public tours/tastings,
            Special events

The Peller family originally planned to open a winery in Ontario in 1961, but unfortunately the government would not grant them a license because the thought at the time was that there were enough wineries already in the region. Undaunted, the Pellers opened their winery in British Columbia where they prospered very nicely making sweet specialty wines under the Andres label.

In 1970, an existing winery in Ontario went up for sale. The Pellers purchased it and then proceeded to extend their winery holdings to five Canadian provinces and over one and a half million gallons of wine production by 1995. Alberta, British Columbia, Nova Scotia, Ontario and Québec are all homes for Peller family winery property.

Over the years, the Pellers recognized that consumer tastes were gradually changing from their product line of sweet specialty wines to drier table wines that better complemented food. To accommodate the consumer, a new line of premium varietal wines was created and introduced to the public a few years ago. Peller Estates wines have now achieved the VQA (Vintners Quality Alliance) designation and are the showcase of Andres/Peller Estates.

The attractive tasting room and boutique at Andres/Peller Estates in Winona, Ontario, is noted for its informative tours, hospitable guides and generous tasting samples. Tours include the cellars and bottling facilities and last about a half to three quarters of an hour before concluding at the tasting bar. Tour schedules may vary slightly during the busy seasons, so it is recommended to call to confirm times. Tastings of the Andres/Peller Estates wines are always available during regular hours and the hospitality room is available for private tours and functions by reservation.

The Peller family may not have been able to get their winery business started in Ontario in 1961, but they overcame the obstacles to become one of Canada's largest winery companies in the 1990's.

Brights/Cartier

LOCATION: 4887 Dorchester Road
Niagara Falls, Ontario L2E 6N8
(905) 357-2400

TOUR TIMES: May through October
10:30 AM, 2 PM & 3:30 PM, Mon.-Sat.
2 PM & 3:30 PM on Sundays

November through April
2 PM, Mon.- Fri
2 PM & 3:30 PM, Sat. & Sun.

AMENITIES: Tours & tasting, Retail store

Brights/Cartier is part of the newly-formed conglomerate Vincor International, Inc. that has now become the eighth largest winery operation in North America. T.G. Brights and Cartier were successful companies in their own right and their wine labels were well-known to Canadian residents. To enter the fast-growing global market, however, the two brands merged, acquired the Inniskillin Winery and developed a new vintage-dated selection of varietal wines marketed under the label of Jackson Triggs. With 130 retail outlets selling over 95 different brands of their own products and over 2 million gallons of production, the giant wine company is now in a state of transition to organize itself into an efficient, smooth-running enterprise.

Other brands in the corporate portfolio include L'Ambiance, Capistro and President Champagne, one of Canada's most famous sparkling wines. Their Sawmill Creek line is unusual in that bulk wines are imported from the United States, Chile and other countries, then combined with Ontario wines to form an international blend of wines. All of the company's products and brands are available at any of the stores in the Brights/Cartier retail chain.

At the Brights "Tour Centre" in Niagara Falls, visitors can take a guided tour (about 1 hour) of the old Brights winemaking facilities. Although most of today's winemaking activities take place next door at the huge new state-of-the-art winery, there is plenty of history and technology to see on the walking tour including a museum room featuring authentic winemaking equipment from the previous century. At the conclusion of the tour, visitors are escorted to the Winewood hospitality room where once stood two massive 68,000 gallon wooden tanks. These tanks now form the walls of the Winewood Room that surround guests while they partake in a wine tasting.

Vincor International and Brights/Cartier is a unique blend of Canada's oldest, largest and now one of its newest wineries.

Cave Spring Cellars

LOCATION: 3836 Main Street
            Jordan, Ontario L0R 1S0
            (905) 562-3581 - Winery
            (905) 562-7313 - Restaurant

HOURS: 10 AM - 5 PM, Mon.- Sat.
            Noon - 5 PM, Sunday
            Restaurant open Tues.- Sun.
            for lunch & dinner

AMENITIES: Tasting & retail boutique,
            Winery restaurant

Cave Spring Cellars derives its name from an old Indian legend that tells of a lost limestone cave somewhere in the area that contained a natural spring which was used as a mineral bath. No one knows if such a cave really exists, but if it is ever found the Pennachetti family will surely incorporate it into their winery/restaurant complex on Jordan's Main street.

Since 1986, Leonard Pennachetti has nurtured his fascination for wine production with highly regarded Riesling, Gewurztraminer and Chardonnay white wines. His accomplishments have been noteworthy, particularly in bringing home a Silver Medal for Cave Spring's 100% Riesling Icewine from the prestigious VinExpo '93 in Bordeaux. Many experts feel the Cave Spring's Icewine is the best in Ontario, a region fast becoming world-renowned for this style of wine. In the red category, Gamay Noir, Pinot Noir and a pleasing Cabernet/Merlot blend are also attracting wine enthusiasts. According to Pennachetti, "The winery's philosophy from the outset has been to capture the particular *goût de terroir* (taste of the soil) of the vineyards found along the Beamsville Bench of the Niagara Escarpment."

Most recently, Pennachetti's attention has been focused on another "taste of the soil." In 1993, part of the original Jordan Winery building (circa 1870's) was transformed into Ontario's first, and currently one of its finest, winery-operated restaurant. "On the Twenty" (the restaurant commands a picturesque view overlooking the Twenty Mile Creek running through town) features many locally originated fresh products and a newly developed Niagara cuisine created from the skill and imagination of celebrated Ontario chef Michael Olson. According to Pennachetti, "What Michael does in the restaurant precisely mirrors what we do in the cellar and the parallel extends to the results: superlative cuisine to match our award-winning wines."

Cave Spring Cellars and On the Twenty Restaurant have gained notoriety quite rapidly and are the center attraction in this historic town that offers a number of shops from antiques to a teddy bear factory. **123**

Chateau des Charmes
Winery & Vineyards

LOCATION: 1025 York Road
St. Davids, Ontario L0S 1P0
(905) 262-4210

HOURS: 9 AM to 6 PM, daily

AMENITIES: Tasting room & boutique,
Video presentation,
Group and public tours,
Private banquet facilities

There is no winery structure in Ontario that is more majestic than the imposing edifice at Château des Charmes. Easily accessible off the Q.E.W. highway, this magnificent new building is set within an immaculate 85-acre vineyard and seductively beckons all who venture near to succumb to their curiosity.

From the moment you pass through the distinctive entryway, you know you are witnessing a winery masterpiece. A huge glass chandelier sparkles in the light above the French door entrance to the "Theatre" where an informative 15-minute video presentation takes place. Next, admiring visitors cross the grand foyer bound for a walking tour of the state-of-the-art winemaking facilities, the barrel aging room and then finish in the tasting room dominated by the presence of an exquisite oak wine bar. After sampling a number of the Château's expertly made wines, guests are invited to the adjoining boutique for wine and gift purchases.

The experience and ambiance of Château des Charmes is so dazzling that one would easily forgive the wine if it were not as impressive as its home. However, impeccable quality reigns supreme at Château des Charmes from the grounds to the bottle and the wines are the crowning glory of the Bosc family. Through six generations of French winemakers, the family fine-tuned their skill and technology. Now they have built a splendid facility.

The Bosc family believes that the finest wines can only be made from the finest grapes, so they have concentrated on the classic European varieties of Chardonnay, Pinot Noir, Cabernet Sauvignon, Merlot, Cabernet Franc and Riesling. As a result of their dedication to quality, Château des Charmes wines have earned nearly 100 awards in national and international competitions.

The estate of Château des Charmes is a showcase for expertly crafted wines that bring honor and recognition to a dedicated family. As the Paul Bosc family proudly states, "Our new château is a modern rendition of an old world tradition." And, it's an awesome accomplishment!

124

Colio Wines

LOCATION: 1 Colio Drive
Harrow, Ontario N0R 1G0
(519) 738-2241

HOURS: 10 AM to 5 PM, Mon.-Sat.
Open Sundays in December

AMENITIES: Tasting room & gift shop,
Walking tour of facility

A rapidly growing wine region of Ontario is the Lake Erie North Shore near Windsor. The influx of casino gambling in Windsor has had a favorable effect on tourism in the area and has generated a renewed interest in developing winery tasting rooms in order to attract visitors.

For Colio, the interest in Lake Erie North Shore wines began with their wine master, Carlo Negri, who honed his craft for seventeen years in the Trentino Alto-Adiege region of Northern Italy. Negri supervised the first "crush" at Colio in 1980 and has combined the last fifteen years of productivity with his experience in his native Italy to create a formidable line of wines.

Colio's production of over 125,000 cases ranks them as one of the largest wineries in the region. Although they purchase many of the grapes used for their wines, they also maintain over 100 acres of vineyards in South West Ontario. The vineyards are situated in an area location the same latitude as Northern California and that of the Chianti Classico region in Italy.

Besides the winery and the vineyards, Colio operates 15 retail outlets throughout the Province. To support this ambitious venture Colio turns out an extensive line of wine products from value-oriented house table wines to VQA premium varietal wines. Colio also produces two sparkling wines in the charmat method (bulk process). The Chateau D'Or brand is made up of 80% Riesling and 20% Chardonnay, is semi-dry and works well as a satisfying aperitif. The Colio Spumante (Italian terminology used for referring to sparkling wine) is 90% Vidal and 10% Muscat grapes to give it a pleasant, fruity, semi-sweet flavor not unlike Italy's Asti Spumante.

The winery hospitality room is the final destination of an informative tour of the facility and allows one to sample, discuss and purchase any of the wines in the complete line. The retail outlets offer an array of services including custom labeling, gift packaging, food and wine consultation or...just a nice bottle of Colio wine to take home.

Culotta Winery

LOCATION: 1185 North Service Rd. E.
Oakville, Ontario
(905) 844-7912

HOURS: 9 AM to 6 PM, Mon. - Fri.
10 AM to 6 PM, Sat.
Noon to 5 PM, Sunday

AMENITIES: Tasting & self-guided tours,
Multiple retail locations

Like many Ontario wineries, Culotta is an outgrowth of a prosperous grape and juice company. Peter Culotta founded the winery in 1979 and located it in Oakville near the lucrative Toronto market. Since Culotta was already in the grape and juice trade, it seemed like a good business decision to expand into wine.

Although the area around Toronto is a profitable wine market, the region is not conducive to grape-growing. Culotta brings in grapes and juice from literally around the world. Their VQA wines are produced from grapes grown in the vineyards around the Niagara region and brought to the winery for crushing, fermentation and final processing of the juice into wine. It is at this point that the uniqueness of Culotta wines stand out. Culotta offers a blended line of wines which combine Ontario wines with bulk wines made from imported grapes and juices from California to South Africa. This international line of popular-priced wines, in conjunction with the 100% Ontario VQA wines, gives Culotta a fresh marketing approach and a diverse inventory for wine consumers.

From an excellent example of Seyval Blanc to a big, fruity Gewürztraminer and from a barrel-fermented Chardonnay to economical 5 and 16 liter packages of blended wines, Culotta maintains a wide spectrum of choices for customers of its six retail outlets located throughout the province.

After three generations in the grape business and expansion into commercial winemaking, Culotta still continues to be a major supplier of juice for home winemakers and has dedicated a full-time staff member to assist and answer questions on winemaking, plus the winery maintains a library of winemaking reference books.

Visitors to the Culotta Winery have the opportunity to examine the self-guided tour display complete with a video presentation explaining the entire winemaking process from vineyard to bottle. Guests then sample many of the Culotta wines including the specialty wines of Vidal Icewine, Premium Champagne and Amore Sparkling wine.

D'Angelo Estate Winery

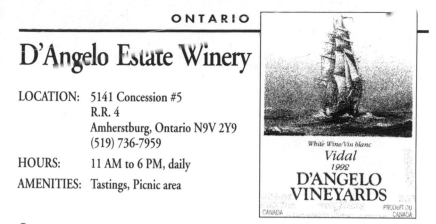

White Wine/Vin blanc
Vidal
1992
D'ANGELO
VINEYARDS
CANADA
PRODUIT DU
CANADA

LOCATION: 5141 Concession #5
R.R. 4
Amherstburg, Ontario N9V 2Y9
(519) 736-7959

HOURS: 11 AM to 6 PM, daily

AMENITIES: Tastings, Picnic area

Salvatore D'Angelo is a winemaker...and a pretty good one at that. But D'Angelo is also a man of the earth. Some might call him a grape farmer, others, who recognize his talents, refer to him as a viticulturist, one who practices both the art and the science of grape-growing.

D'Angelo believes that the true quality of premium wine begins in the vineyards and that's where he puts his signature effort. He explains that the key to sound, ripe grapes comes from the soil and lots of sunshine. D'Angelo developed a sophisticated system of trellising for the vines called "divided canopies" which involves the use of a complicated scheme of wires to train the vines to grow in a "U" shape. By incorporating this method the grapes receive the maximum amount of sunlight and air contact which allows the grapes to grow to their full potential.

When a viticulturist is also the winemaker and is proficient in the skills of both functions, he is then technically called a "viniculturist." The terminology, however, is much more complicated than either the man or his winery. A small family operation, the D'Angelo's winery, offices and tasting area are under one roof of a large barn and D'Angelo still uses such "low-tech" equipment as noise alarms in the vineyards to frighten the birds from eating the grapes. When it comes to nature, a conscientious man utilizes the most effective approach without creating disharmony.

The D'Angelo wines are well-made, straightforward and natural products of the land without a lot of fanfare or marketing pizzazz. The one exception is the Annual D'Angelo Barbecue and Wine Tasting to celebrate the coming of the new harvest. Nearly 1,000 people show up in late August each year to join in the festivities.

To get to the D'Angelo Estate Winery, however, you must take care to follow your map. As of this writing, the convenient "Wine Route" signs found on the Niagara Peninsula are not as prevalent in this Lake Erie region. Hopefully, that will change soon.

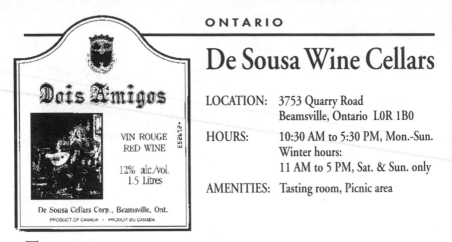

De Sousa Wine Cellars

LOCATION: 3753 Quarry Road
            Beamsville, Ontario L0R 1B0

HOURS: 10:30 AM to 5:30 PM, Mon.-Sun.
            Winter hours:
            11 AM to 5 PM, Sat. & Sun. only

AMENITIES: Tasting room, Picnic area

To reach De Sousa Wine Cellars you must keep a sharp eye on your map and the "Wine Route" signs. You do not want to miss this very unique winery which leads you into another time and culture. As you make your way on to Quarry Road off Highway 8 and approach the striking red-tiled roof building that houses the De Sousa Cellars, you get the sensation you have arrived at a European countryside estate. As you enter the classic Mediterranean structure you begin to narrow down the location to Spain or Portugal. Within minutes of being greeted by one of the engaging De Sousa family members, you are informed that Portugal is indeed your port-of-call.

In the corner of the new, but "old world" room, is a magnificent 18th century wine press brought here by John De Sousa, Sr. from his family's estate on the island of St. Michael, just off the coast of Portugal. The walls are adorned with hand-painted ceramic tiles and an unglazed bowl is offered to sample your wine. The unglazed goblets and bowls are traditional Portuguese vessels for consuming wine and are a trademark of the winery.

John De Sousa, Sr. arrived in Ontario over thirty years ago and opened a restaurant. In 1979, he purchased the 77-acre farm and vineyards in Beamsville. In 1987, when the wholesale grape market began to evaporate, De Sousa began making wine like his family did for generations in Portugal. In 1992, he built the edifice that now stands as a tribute to his ethnic heritage.

De Sousa makes excellent wines from Cabernet Franc, Chardonnay, Cabernet Sauvignon and a Vidal Icewine, but the heart of the De Sousa Wine Cellars is the traditional Portuguese styled *Dois Amigos* in red and white. Locals are constantly seen coming and going with all they can carry on a regular basis. While you're there, ask if they make a *porto* style wine. They do, but it is very limited, not always available and absolutely magnificent.

Henry of Pelham Estate Winery

LOCATION: 1469 Pelham Road
St. Catharines, Ontario L2R 6P7
(905) 684-8423

HOURS: 10 AM to 6 PM, daily
Year round

AMENITIES: Tasting room and tours, Picnic area,
Private facilities,
Special events during summer

In 1794, Nicholas Smith was awarded a land grant in Canada for his dedicated service to the crown. Smith guaranteed a family tradition and legacy for his land by fathering fourteen children and the family never lost sight of its obligation. In 1842, his son Henry, known as Henry of Pelham in the official archives, built Henry Smith's Inn & Tollgate which served as a focal point for the community over the next 100 years.

Today, two of those descendants, Paul and Matthew Speck, have fully restored the old Inn to house the Henry of Pelham winery tasting room, boutique and banquet facilities. Upon entering the downstairs tasting room one has the feeling of setting foot in an old English wine cellar. But in actuality, the lower level room was the kitchen for the original Inn and visitors may still observe the same huge brick oven that baked bread for the customers upstairs.

The Speck brothers recently celebrated the 200th anniversary of the land grant and the first planting of grapevines in the region by Henry and Nicholas Smith. Their vineyards of Chardonnay and Baco Noir are the mainstay of winery sales, but fine examples of Cabernet Sauvignon/Merlot, Vidal, Chenin Blanc and Riesling wines are also enjoyed by visitors. The Specks have dedicated their efforts to carry on the long family tradition as "a new generation of creative farmers, vintners and professionals." They do so by producing small batches of hand-crafted premium wines that have gained numerous awards and international recognition...plus they have fun doing it.

The staff of Henry of Pelham are excellent hosts for weddings, private dinners and informative winery tours that are conducted three times daily. During the busy summer months the estate is often the site for weekend barbecues, food and wine festivals and numerous other events where locals and tourists alike gather for good food, excellent wine and camaraderie. It seems as if the old Henry Smith Tavern and Inn never closed...it just got better!

129

Hernder Estate Winery

LOCATION: 1607 8th Avenue
St. Catharines, Ontario L2R 6P7
(905) 684-3300

HOURS: 10 AM to 6 PM, Mon.-Sat.
11 AM to 5 PM, Sunday

AMENITIES: Tasting room, Hospitality room

Some wineries have interesting histories, others have impressive facilities and yet others have wonderfully esthetic grounds. The Hernder Estate Winery has all of these and more. Approaching the winery on the horizon off Highway 8, one is awestruck by the striking presence of a massive 127 year old restored barn. As the picture unfolds, the larger than life scene becomes even more breathtaking with its expansive grounds of stocked ponds, manicured landscaping and stone-walled fences. The interior of the magnificent structure is just as impressive with a well-appointed tasting room/gift shop, hospitality room and an adjoining modern winery...and the place isn't even finished yet!

Continuing this extraordinary endeavor, already over seven years in the making, future plans call for a full-service restaurant, additions to the already beautiful outdoor panorama such as a covered bridge, gazebos, special public events and dozens of other marketing ideas that will call attention to the Hernder Winery and its wines.

Ah, yes, the wines. The Hernder family has been tending their 500 acre farm for three generations. Over 250 acres of the family land is devoted to premium grape varieties for the production of wine which only began with the establishment of the winery in 1993. But when the Hernders make up their minds to do something, they go all out. Currently Riesling and Chardonnay lead the Hernder tasting list accompanied by Seyval, Vidal and, of course, an Icewine. Winemaker Ray Cornell also oversees a limited production of Cabernet Franc, Cabernet Sauvignon and Merlot which is often blended together and oak aged as a house red cuvee table wine. Vineyard plantings are expanded each year and the winery's repertoire is sure to grow as well.

The Hernder Estate Winery is not only impressive and a tribute to the family's enterprising vision, but it is also destined to become one of Ontario's premier showcase wineries and will undoubtedly become a "must see" on everyone's itinerary along the "Winery Route."

Hillebrand Estates Winery

LOCATION: R.R. 2, Highway 55
Niagara-on-the-Lake, Ontario L0S 1J0
(905) 468-3201

HOURS: 10 AM to 6 PM, daily

AMENITIES: Tasting room & boutique,
Winery tours

Hillebrand Estates Winery is one of the larger wineries in Ontario (over 300,000 cases) and offers one of the most complete visitor winery tour programs in the Province. The one-hour excursion includes the entire winery, inside and out, from the vineyard to the press house, aging cellars and barrel room.

Due to the vastness of their production, Hillebrand Estates has created a computer program to analyze and track the grape production from each of its vineyards and winegrowers. This enables Hillebrand's capable winemakers to create a three tier level of products to meet consumers' varying needs and pocketbooks.

The "Harvest Classic" series has gained recognition for its quality value and consistent varietal character which proves to be very "food friendly" for daily consumption. The Harvest Classic series is made up of a Chardonnay, Riesling, Pinot Gris, Gewürztraminer, Muscat Reserve and a Gamay Noir. The "Collectors' Choice" wines of barrel-aged Chardonnay and Cabernet/ Merlot are created for the patient connoisseur who wishes to cellar a fine wine and follow its maturation. These wines are aged at the winery for a minimum of 18 months and benefit from additional storage. The "Trius Series" are Hillebrand's top echelon wines, hand-crafted by their winemakers. This series includes a distinctive blend of Cabernet Sauvignon, Merlot and Cabernet Franc patterned after the classic Bordeaux blends of France. The Trius Chardonnay is a blend of three premium estates to maximize fruit aromas and flavors. The final Trius is a delicate Riesling designed with a dry, crisp finish which should complement fresh fish or seafood dishes very nicely.

Two specialty products are also expertly crafted by Hillebrand, the "Mounier Brut" and, of course, another famous Ontario Icewine. The sparkling wine is made in the classic *methode champenoise* of bottle fermentation and is ideally suited for before, during or after a meal. The aromatic dessert wine of frozen grapes has, like most of Ontario's Icewines, brought recognition to the area for its production of this unique and rare product.

Inniskillin Wines

LOCATION: R.R. 1
(on Line 3 off the Niagara Parkway)
Niagara-on-the-Lake, Ontario L0S 1J0
(905) 468-3554

HOURS: 10 AM to 6 PM, daily
10 AM to 5 PM, Nov.-April

AMENITIES: Wine bar & Boutique,
Self-guided & public tours,
Art Gallery, Chef's seminars

The name Inniskillin is derived from an old Irish military regiment named the Inniskilling Fusiliers who served during the War of 1812. Colonel Cooper, a member of that Inniskilling regiment, was granted crown land in Canada, part of which eventually became the site of the original Inniskillin Winery.

Set in the middle of vineyards with an approaching drive lined with large wooden wine barrels, your expectations for a very special visit begin to rise as you enter the estate. The boutique is located in an old restored barn, but don't let the outside barnwood appearance fool you. The interior, which houses the retail shop, an art gallery loft and an accommodating staff, is of modern design and geared for contemporary retailing. The winery is also state-of-the-art and produces an excellent stable of wines including limited bottlings of "vineyard select" premium varieties.

Inniskillin has developed a "self-guided tour" format that is organized by various stations throughout the property. Each station is well-illustrated and describes in detail all aspects of viticulture (grape growing) and enology (science of winemaking). The tour begins in the small barn building where you can read about the winery's history, climate, soil, geography, harvesting and even the history of the wine cork. At your leisure you follow the marked path through twenty different stations of the facility and all phases of the winemaking process. Informative guided tours are also available daily during the summer and on weekends from November through May. All the tours conclude in the Wine Boutique where you can examine the current display of art in the loft, watch winemaking videos, taste expertly made wine or "shop to your heart's content."

With a little planning you can also participate in one of the many special activities scheduled in the summer and fall, including chef demonstrations, art and exhibits and book signings. Inniskillin Winery is definitely a "must stop" along the scenic Niagara Parkway.

Kittling Ridge Estate Wines & Spirits

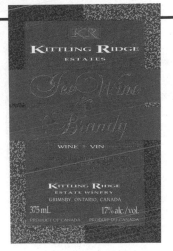

LOCATION: 297 South Service Road
Grimsby, Ontario L3M 4E9
(905) 945-9225

HOURS: 10 AM to 5 PM, Mon.-Sat.
Noon to 5 PM, Sundays

AMENITIES: Tasting room & retail store,
Tours of winery and distillery,
Special events on a monthly basis

Kittling Ridge Estate Wines & Spirits possesses a number of distinctions in Canada's wine and spirits trade. It is the country's *only* winery/distillery operation. It is the *only* company that produces a Canadian brandy. It opened the *first* on-premise distillery retail store in Ontario. More noteworthy, however, is Kittling Ridge's development of a completely unique wine product, different from almost anything else in the world.

Proprietor John Hall, a winemaker for over 25 years, was already utilizing the abundance of premium, tender fruit from the Niagara Peninsula by making a number of excellent fruit-flavored brandies and *eau de vie* (concentrated distilled fruit wine), but he was searching for an distinctive wine product that would serve as a "signature" item for his winery.

With the international success of Ontario's Icewine and his newly acquired distillery, experimentation naturally followed to blend Icewine and brandy, an idea similar to the French Pineau de Charente which is a blend of white wine and Cognac. Hall recognized that the Icewine of the area was excellent and was achieving more recognition everyday, but everyone was making it and he felt it was a bit too sweet. To differentiate his Icewine from the rest of the pack, brandy was introduced to it. The outcome was a tasting room hit for "Icewine & Brandy." His next step was to create an *eau de vie* from Icewine and blend it back into the undistilled portion of the wine. The resulting sensation of "Icewine & Eau de Vie" serves as a superb apéritif or dessert wine that offers an intense fruit flavor without being syrupy sweet. It actually complements a meal of fresh shrimp, crab or lobster very nicely.

Kittling Ridge Estate Wines & Spirits has not only two of the most unique wine products in the world, but John Hall has created two winners that will gain international fame for the enterprising proprietor as soon as the word spreads... and that won't take long!

Konzelmann Estate Winery

LOCATION: R.R. 3, 1096 Lakeshore Rd.
Niagara-on-the-Lake, Ontario L0S 1J0
(905) 935-2866

HOURS: 10 AM to 6 PM, Mon.-Sat.
12:30 to 5:30 PM, Sunday
Closed Sundays, Jan.-April

AMENITIES: Tasting room

The German Konzelmann family has been making wine since 1893, though it was in 1984 that the fourth and fifth generations of Konzelmann's emigrated to Canada and promptly created a winery in the family tradition. The German influence of the Konzelmann family is very evident from the attractive "old world" tasting room and retail shop on Lakeshore Road to the vertical trellising of the vineyards that expand to the shore of Lake Ontario.

Konzelmann has built its reputation on the production of Johannisberg Riesling-based wines with a delightful spectrum ranging from dry to sweet. According to German quality winemaking, superior wines are sweetened by their own natural juice and not with sugar. The Konzelmann's hold true to this traditional winemaking process and allow the land and the Lake Ontario climate to guide their efforts in achieving the wine's balance and full flavor. In this era of total mechanization, the family and staff even pick many of their grapes the "old world" way...by hand.

Konzelmann also produces Chardonnay, Pinot Blanc and Pinot Noir varietal wines among others. Five acres of the 40-acre farm is devoted to "trial varieties" to determine the extent that the winery may branch out while maintaining the important VQA designation and family standard of quality control.

Gewürztraminer is another specialty of Konzelmann, this German/Alsatian grape variety is slated for expanded planting for production of the characteristic spicy wine it yields. Vinified slightly sweet, in the German tradition, this excellent wine can be enjoyed on its own or with sharp cheese and desserts.

Of course, no German heritage winery would be complete without the addition of a German and Canadian specialty...Icewine. Konzelmann's version has good character and luscious sweetness.

The Konzelmann's take great pride in their family's tradition of grapegrowing and winemaking, but are also committed "to play a leading role in the development of methods that will shape the future of winemaking in Canada."

Lakeview Cellars Estate Winery

LOCATION: 4037 Cherry Avenue
             Vineland, Ontario L0R 2C0

HOURS: 10 AM to 5:30 PM, Mon.-Sun.
          (More limited hours during the winter)

AMENITIES: Tasting/retail room, Picnic area

Like many winemakers in the Great Lakes Region, Eddy Gurinskas began making wine as a hobby in his home. After 35 years of notoriety for his amateur accomplishments, he and his wife, Lorraine opened Lakeview Cellars. The Gurinskas home and winery is surrounded by ten acres of vineyards consisting of Baco Noir, Cabernet Sauvignon, Chardonnay, Pinot Gris and Vidal.

The Gurinskas' established the Lakeview Cellars Estate Winery in 1991 and Eddy designed and built the winery building which also houses the retail store and offers a comfortable loft overlooking Lake Ontario for group tastings. The first year production of Lakeview Cellars was only 1,300 cases, but the Gurinskas' plan on reaching their production capacity of 5,000 cases in the near future. They will be supplementing their own estate-grown grapes with varieties such as Riesling and Pinot Noir purchased from neighboring vineyards.

Lakeview Cellars is truly a "mom and pop" winery with the couple's involvement in every phase of the operation. Eddy serves as both the winemaker and viticulturist, working the fields daily throughout the year until all the grapes are brought in for crushing and distributed to the fermentation and aging tanks. Eddy and Lorraine both work the retail outlet as well, scurrying back and forth from the winery office and the continuous paperwork. It's hard work, but one the Gurinskas' obviously love.

The Gurinskas' "labor of love" has also earned the wines of Lakeview Cellars the designation "VQA" which is Canada's equivalent of the various *appellation controllée* that exist in wine countries such as France (A.O.C.), Germany (QmP) and Italy (DOC). The "Vintners Quality Alliance" certifies that the wines have been tasted and approved by an independent quality control panel and have achieved the quality standards set forth by the VQA.

This designation is not taken lightly in Canada and consumers have come to rely on the VQA seal for quality control. For Lakeview Cellars, the VQA Gold Medallion status was awarded for their specialty Icewine and Cabernet Sauvignon products. That's a long way from home winemaking!

LeBlanc Estate Winery

LOCATION: 4716 Concession # 4, R.R. 2
Harrow, Ontario N0R 1G0
(519) 738-9228

HOURS: 11 AM to 6 PM, Tues.-Sat.
1 PM to 5 PM, Sunday
Closed Mondays

AMENITIES: Tasting room, Bulk juice supply

Lyse LeBlanc is a very capable and hard working winemaker who learned her trade the hard way...on-the-job training. Lyse and her husband Pierre have been tending their 120 acre grape farm since 1983 and selling their fruit to neighboring wineries. The increasing demand for their quality Vidal, Riesling and Seyval grapes and juices prompted Lyse to try her hand at making some LeBlanc Estate wines from part of their crop. By 1993, the LeBlanc children were old enough for Lyse to commit additional time to the family business. The LeBlancs were granted a winery license and a new family farm winery was established in the Lake Erie North Shore Region, near Windsor.

No sooner had Lyse LeBlanc built up a pretty good wine and juice trade from her winery retail shop than the severe winter of '94 hit and devastated most of the vinifera grape crop. It was a struggle for the small operation and LeBlanc was forced to curtail wine production until the vines recovered the following year.

Some of her excellent Riesling, Vidal and Pinot Blanc is still available at the winery along with a very limited supply of attractive hand-painted bottles of Vidal Icewine. The price of the LeBlanc Icewine is not inexpensive, but it is worth the investment just to experience this luscious dessert wine.

LeBlanc produces a creditable Chardonnay and Gewürztraminer from grapes purchased from a nearby grower. She has also crafted an attractive Cabernet Franc and Cabernet Sauvignon blend and is developing a Pinot Blanc wine from the LeBlanc estate.

A big part of LeBlanc revenue is still generated by a loyal clientele of home winemakers who depend on Lyse LeBlanc for premium quality grape juice. In the fall, there is a steady parade of buyers bringing in their empty carboys and tanks to be filled by LeBlanc while they confer on the results of the most recent harvest and the potential of their soon-to-be wine for next year's consumption.

At times the grape growing and winemaking business can be a trying experience, but Lyse LeBlanc enjoys the challenge and creative outlet.

London Winery — Cedar Springs Vineyards

CEDAR SPRINGS
WINES

Proprietors Reserve
1991
DeCHAUNAC

RED WINE ❦ VIN ROUGE
11.5% alc./vol.   750 mL
VQA ONTARIO VQA

LOCATION: London Winery
540 Wharncliffe Road S.
London, Ontario N6J 2N5
(519) 686-8431

Cedar Springs Vineyards
at Eastman's Market
Highway 3 (just west of Blenheim,
Ontario)
(519) 676-8008

HOURS: 10 AM to 6 PM, Mon.-Thurs. & Sat.
10 AM to 9 PM, Fridays
Noon to 6 PM, Sundays

AMENITIES: Tastings and tours, Picnic facilities at Cedar Springs

London Winery Limited is somewhat of an enigma. It is one of oldest, largest and most successful family winery operations in Ontario, but has only recently opened its hallowed halls to the public. In 1993, the third genera tion Knowles brothers decided to allow tours of the winemaking facilities for the first time in its nearly 70-year history by building an impressive $1.5 million, 15,000 sq. ft. touring center adjacent to the winery.

Guests may now examine the history of the company, view winery memorabilia and take in a comprehensive explanation of vineyard management and winemaking in the audio-visual theater. There is a charge for each of the three tour and tasting packages that include cheese and crackers with a selection of wines, but they are worth the price of admission.

The Cedar Springs Vineyards tasting room, some 60 miles west of the London winemaking facility, is more casual as it sits next to a roadside market and entertains its visitors with a vineyard tour and then a tasting in a converted 10,000 gallon redwood barrel aptly named "The Barrel Room." The Cedar Springs estate supplies the premium vinifera and French hybrid grapes for the winery's Proprietor's Reserve wines that have achieved the VQA (Vintners Quality Alliance) designation.

London Winery Limited also operates more than twenty retail outlets and offers an extensive selection of wine products from a superb Icewine to a unique Mead (honey wine) and an array of table and varietal wines that is sure to please most any individual's palate.

Magnotta Winery

1992
RIESLING
Medium Dry
WHITE WINE   VIN BLANC
750 ml   11% alc./vol.
PRODUCT OF CANADA   PRODUIT DU CANADA
MAGNOTTA WINERY   VAUGHAN   ONTARIO   CANADA

LOCATIONS: 110 Cidermill Ave.
Vaughan, Ontario L4K 4L9
(905) 738-9463

2555 Dixie Road at Dundas
Mississauga, Ontario L4Y 2A1
(905) 897-9463

4701 Ontario Street
Beamsville, Ontario L0R 1B4
(905) 563-5313

HOURS: 10 AM to 6 PM, Daily (Hours vary
between stores and seasons)

AMENITIES: Tasting, tours & retail shop,
Home winemaking supplies

The Magnotta Winery is a multi-faceted and intriguing operation. Gabe and Rossana Magnotta oversee a winery, a selection of choice vineyard lands and multiple retail stores. They're also juice purveyors for home winemakers, importers of international wines and juices, exporters of Ontario Icewine and patrons of the arts. As if that wasn't enough to keep the energetic couple busy, they have also applied for beer and spirits licenses to "diversify" their company...and they have only been in business a little over 10 years!

It all began in 1984 when the Magnottas started their juice importing company called Festa Juices. They became very successful supplying home winemakers with quality juices from the world's fine wine-growing regions. Soon they decided to get into the wine business themselves and bought a winery property in Vaughan (just north of Toronto) and created the Magnotta Winery. Shortly after that, they found there was no room for their wine on the LCBO (Liquor Control Board of Ontario) retail shelves, so they elected to enter the retail market through their own stores (now three and soon-to-be four locations).

The Magnottas also introduced a couple of unique twists to their marketing strategy. Using their experience in the juice importing business, they began blending Ontario wines (25%) with products from Italy, Chile, California, Washington and Oregon to create an International Series of wines in addition to their regular lines of Ontario varietals and blended wines. They then commissioned international artists to create a variety of artwork to be utilized on their labels. The results have been phenomenally successful and have gained international recognition for the Magnottas' attractively-priced wines.

138

Marynissen Estates

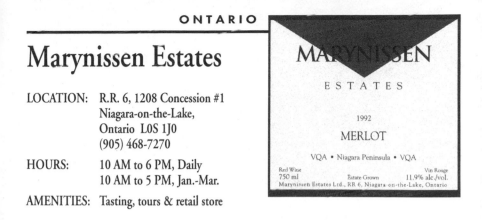

LOCATION: R.R. 6, 1208 Concession #1
                 Niagara-on-the-Lake,
                 Ontario L0S 1J0
                 (905) 468-7270

HOURS: 10 AM to 6 PM, Daily
                 10 AM to 5 PM, Jan.-Mar.

AMENITIES: Tasting, tours & retail store

At age sixty-five, when most hard-working men turn their attention to a nice cozy condo on a warm-weather golf course, John Marynissen decided to open a winery. Not only did he build his winery in a cool temperate zone, but he also chose to specialize in a warm climate grape variety - Cabernet Sauvignon. In 1990 when many people thought Marynissen was losing his faculties, he entered the realm of uncertainty with the full support of his family.

John Marynissen arrived in Canada in 1952 from the Netherlands. After a year of picking fruit and other miscellaneous jobs he took his first risk in this "New World" by buying a small farm. It was difficult at first adjusting to the land that was so different than what he had known in Europe. But John was a fast learner and his wife, Nanny, was a patient supporter. Eventually, Marynissen began growing grapes and over the next few decades became renowned for the quality of his products as wineries produced award-winning wines from the grapes of his vineyards. He even tried his hand at home-winemaking and began dominating amateur competitions. By 1990 he wasn't anywhere near retiring and his three children encouraged him to exploit his grape-growing and winemaking talents and open a commercial winery. Today, Marynissen Estates is singled out when writers and winemakers cite an example of how winemaking success can be achieved against the odds.

Marynissen Estates now offers excellent examples of Chardonnay, Riesling and Gewürztraminer, but the focus is still on red wines (approximately 70% of the total production) with Cabernet Sauvignon, Merlot, Gamay and Pinot Noir dominating the tasting room conversation.

Marynissen Estates winery is a small (5-6,000 cases) family-run boutique winery and is located just off the scenic Niagara Parkway. To experience something out of the norm for this wine region, don't miss visiting Marynissen and sampling one of Ontario's best (and rare) Cabernet Sauvignons.

Pelee Island Winery

PELEE ISLAND WINERY

Red Wine

Vin Rouge

750 ml

12.0% alc./vol.

Pinot Noir

1991

Estate Bottled By
Pelee Island Winery and Vineyards Inc.
Kingsville, Ontario

Product of Canada

Produit du Canada

LOCATION:	455 Highway 18 East Kingsville, Ontario N94 2L8 (519) 733-6551
HOURS:	9 AM to 6 PM, Mon.-Sat. 10 AM to 5 PM, Sundays Closed Jan.-Mar. Island visits from May to Sept.
AMENITIES:	Retail store & gift shop, Picnic facilities, Tours of mainland winery and Pelee Island

One of the most complete entertainment winery packages in the entire Great Lakes Region is located on Pelee Island in Lake Erie. Starting with the attractive grape arbor entryway to the winery's Hospitality Center, the Pelee Island folks offer an exciting and educational day-outing for the entire family.

The attractive mainland retail store in Kingsville is the beginning of a tasting and winery tour that takes in the complete winemaking facilities highlighted by an informative video presentation. You can sit out on the patio and enjoy the scenery or relax out of the sun at a private table inside the cutout of a mammoth oak wine cask.

The real fun starts at the winery's dock in Kingsville as you board the 265 foot, 7,000 ton M.V. Jiimaan, the largest ferry vessel on Lake Erie. The ferry takes you to Pelee Island where the winery's over 400 acres of European grape varieties thrive on a unique viticultural area that is also home to species of flora and fauna not found in any other location in Canada. A travel tram takes you around the edge of the island to explore the beautiful plants, flowers and lake scenery. You'll pass by remnants of Canada's first successful winery, Vin Villa Ruin and see Pelee Island Lighthouse, the oldest stone lighthouse on Lake Erie.

The tram tour ends at the Wine Pavilion, dotted with picnic tables and gas grills where you can cook your own "buffalo" burger, boneless chicken breast or sausages purchased from the Pavilion's Deli. While the children make the most of the playground facilities, parents can enjoy a peaceful glass of wine or partake in a self-guided tour of the various wine displays set up by the winery.

By the time your afternoon ends on Pelee Island and you return to the mainland, you'll have achieved a greater appreciation of the art of winemaking and the pleasures of life associated with it.

Pillitteri Estates Winery

LOCATION: 1696 Highway 55, R.R. #2
Niagara-on-the-Lake,
Ontario L0S 1J0
(905) 468-3147

HOURS: 10 AM to 8 PM, daily
10 AM to 6 PM, Oct.-April

AMENITIES: Free winery tours & tastings,
Hospitality room,
Art exhibits on the mezzanine,
Farm market and bakery

PILLITTERI
ESTATES WINERY
NIAGARA-ON-THE-LAKE, ONTARIO, CANADA

VQA – ONTARIO – VQA

1992

ICEWINE

SWEET WHITE WINE / VIN BLANC SEC
375 ml.   13.9 % alc./vol.
Product of Canada / Produit du Canada

Pillitteri Estates Winery, Niagara-on-the-Lake, Ontario

For most people who visit the Niagara Peninsula it is a wonderland of natural and man-made beauty. The area is rich with farms, orchards and vineyards inhabited by creative and hard-working people who have captured the spirit and essence of the land and packaged it for all to see. One such person is Gary Pillitteri who created a place that will attract your attention and brighten your spirits, not to mention satisfy your appetite.

For over 20 years, Pillitteri has run a retail farm market and fruit packing plant in the heart of an area that specializes in fruit, vegetables, flowers and plants. In 1992, with the help of family members, Pillitteri decided to extend and revamp his operation. He started by fulfilling a long time dream of owning a winery and building an expansive new facility that would house both his old and new ventures. As plans progressed, a tasting room/boutique was added, plus a hospitality room with seating for 150... plus a mezzanine that overlooks the winery and is used for hosting arts and crafts exhibits...plus a Wine Garden patio set in an orchard...plus a bakery featuring fresh baked breads and desserts...and did I mention a greenhouse with flowers and plants? That, too. Well, it all opened in 1993 and it's definitely not your ordinary farm market winery.

The Pillitteri wines include a number of VQA *vinifera* and French hybrid varietals, grown on the Niagara Peninsula. Though the winery is young, the wines are beginning to garner recognition for the ambitious Pillitteri.

As a visitor, you will have the opportunity to take in all the activity via a structured tour of the facilities, vineyards and orchards or you may wander about on your own, and be sure to have a light lunch in the Wine Garden...you'll need to keep up your strength.

Reif Estate Winery

LOCATION:	15608 Niagara Parkway, R.R. 1
	Niagara-on-the-Lake,
	Ontario L0S 1J0
	(905) 468-7738
HOURS:	10 AM to 6 PM, Daily
AMENITIES:	Tasting room & boutique,
	Tours May-Aug. at 1:30 PM,
	Bed & Breakfast facility

After thirteen generations of winemakers with 300 years of experience, one would think that a winemaking family with such an ancestral background would be well set in their ways. In the case of Germany's Reif family, tradition is limited to quality, beyond that there are no boundaries for expansion and experimentation.

In the 1960's and 70's, Reif family members began scouring the world for a location to build and develop another winery. They came to the Niagara Peninsula and decided this was the area for the family to invest in expansion. Surprisingly, the Reif Estate Winery in Ontario does not specialize in Riesling, the famous German grape variety. In fact, Reif produces more Chardonnay and the French hybrid Vidal than Riesling. Klaus Reif, president and winemaker of the winery, is more educated in the craft of international winemaking than in the traditional German methods and he sees that as fulfillment of his family's dedication to continued excellence in the art of winemaking.

The 135-acre estate does, indeed, grow and produce a significant amount of the Germanic Riesling and Gewürztraminer grapes, but Klaus has diversified the vineyards to include Seyval Blanc, Pinot Noir, Cabernet Sauvignon and Baco Noir. The results of his experiments have resulted in numerous international awards for his wines and the establishment of another world-class winery for the Reif family.

When the Reif family purchased the vineyard land, it included a spectacular mansion (circa 1880) on the scenic Niagara River Parkway. This palatial residence, which displays the opulence and grandiose style typical of the Victorian era, has been converted into a magnificent Bed & Breakfast and has been aptly named "The Grand Victorian." The structure is so dominating that it may occupy your attention as you pass by the entrance next door to the converted stables that now house the Reif winery and tasting room.

Southbrook Farms

LOCATION: 1061 Major MacKenzie Dr.
Maple, Ontario L4C 4X9
(905) 832-2548

HOURS: 9 AM to 6:30 PM, Daily
Winter hours: 11 AM to 4 PM
Fri., Sat. & Sun.

AMENITIES: Tasting and retail room, Full farm
market & bakery, "Pick-your-own"
farm, Weekend barbecues

There are two things one does not expect to see just outside of Toronto's city limits. One is a 200+ acre farm, and the other is a full-fledged winery. But, from the porch of Southbrook Farms' Farm Market/Winery the Toronto skyline and CN Tower are clearly recognizable. It's no wonder that Toronto residents scurry out Route 400 for fresh vegetables, fruit and a couple bottles of Southbrook Farms wine.

The natural progression from the fruit farm business to a functioning winery was the brainchild of Bill Redelmeier, Ian Hanna and Derek Barnett. "We all just got together one day and said, 'Why don't we make wine?' and shortly thereafter, we opened a winery," explains Barnett. "Our first mission, however, was to make grape wine, so we needed to procure grapes from the Niagara Peninsula since our climate is not conducive to grape-growing."

Since that auspicious beginning in 1991 the winery now utilizes grapes and juice from California as well as Niagara and they are blended together in several of the wines. The wines are made in a converted old dairy barn, circa 1890, and sold through the Southbrook Farms' winery tasting room. They produce about 8,000 gallons per year and Barnett says that they will probably level off the production in the 10,000 gallon range.

Southbrook Farms' future growth seems to be with the fruit products they grow on the farm. "We've done very well with fortified dessert wines made from raspberries and black currants," says Barnett, "that seems to be a logical area for us to expand into."

Regardless of Southbrook Farms' growth, there are plenty of attractions for visitors. From "pick-your-own," to fresh farm produce, farm-made jams, jellies and mustards; from one of the 25,000 pies that come fresh out of their bakery ovens annually to weekend farm cookouts, guests can also get a bottle of some pretty good wine, relax and enjoy the lush rolling fields of the country... just outside the city limits.

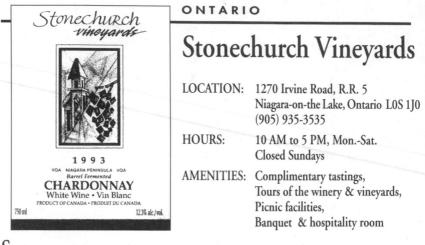

Stonechurch Vineyards

LOCATION: 1270 Irvine Road, R.R. 5
             Niagara-on-the Lake, Ontario L0S 1J0
             (905) 935-3535

HOURS: 10 AM to 5 PM, Mon.-Sat.
             Closed Sundays

AMENITIES: Complimentary tastings,
             Tours of the winery & vineyards,
             Picnic facilities,
             Banquet & hospitality room

Stonechurch Vineyards takes its name from the oldest church in Niagara which is down the road on winery property and is indeed made of stone. The church was established in 1853 and at one time during Prohibition, "rum runners" secretively stored their contraband beneath the building. It is interesting that in later years this same religious stone structure would be surrounded by vineyards and be the namesake for a respected (and legal) family winery operation.

The farming Hunse family migrated to the Niagara area from the Netherlands in the 1950's and began growing grapes for local wineries in the 1970's. In 1990, family members decided to put the "fruits of their labor" into their own bottles and opened the Stonechurch Vineyards winery. Since that time, the Hunses have experienced rapid growth each year, including breaking into the difficult Asian market with their highly regarded Icewine. The Vidal Icewine is a specialty of Stonechurch and is its signature wine. The Hunses produce up to 3,500 liters a year of the delicious dessert nectar. That is an enormous amount of production for this very risky and labor intensive wine product.

The family and staff of Stonechurch Vineyards are especially hospitable and very consumer oriented. Beyond the basic tour of the cellars and bottling line, Stonechurch also offers wagon ride excursions through the vineyards. Here the growing methods and philosophy of the winery are explained to visitors. The enthusiastic staff stresses that, "Stonechurch feels quality starts right here in the vineyards." The facilities are also available for private functions and an outdoor patio is convenient for visitors to take a break from their touring schedule and enjoy a picnic lunch with some Stonechurch wine.

It is obvious by the quality of the product, the eagerness of the staff and the attractiveness of the winery that Stonechurch Vineyards wines are the result of "tender loving care"... and plenty of skill.

Stoney Ridge Cellars

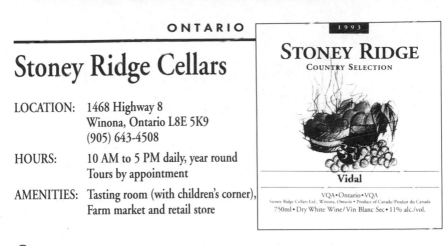

LOCATION: 1468 Highway 8
Winona, Ontario L8E 5K9
(905) 643-4508

HOURS: 10 AM to 5 PM daily, year round
Tours by appointment

AMENITIES: Tasting room (with children's corner),
Farm market and retail store

One of Ontario's most frequently honored wineries lies along the base of the Niagara Escarpment in Winona. Stoney Ridge Cellars is small and unpre tentious, but the portrayal of a simple, old-fashioned farm winery is a clever disguise. Stoney Ridge Cellars is the recipient of numerous wine competition awards from around the world and is heralded for its premium quality and state-of-the-art wine production. Winemaker Jim Warren is well-versed in small-lot crushing, the matching of cultured yeast to various grape varieties and the use of oak barrel treatment which enhances his distinctive style.

The winery operation is on the Puddicombe Farm Estate, home of some of the Stoney Ridge wine grapes and other fruit. The Puddicombe Farm Market on the other side of the Stoney Ridge tasting room is filled with country preserves, fresh fruit in season and plenty of wine-related items.

The excellent wines of Stoney Ridge Cellars are reason enough to warrant a visit, but upon entering the contemporary barn building one is drawn to the aroma of fresh baked goods from the Farm Market side of the building. Even the most focused "oenophile" (wine enthusiast) is easily distracted to a maze of mouth-watering sights and smells.

A stop at Stoney Ridge Cellars and the Puddicombe Farm Market is one of those rare "family" winery destinations. There's even a children's corner in the tasting room where a flurry of coloring activity takes place while parents enjoy the delicate bouquets and lush fruit flavors of the Stoney Ridge wines at the complimentary tasting bar. Once the tantalizing fragrances of the Farm Market overcome the senses (and they will eventually) the family may succumb to lunch on the balcony or patio while enjoying the surrounding landscape scenery.

Be advised, however, that a visit to Stoney Ridge Cellars and Puddicombe Farm Market *will* result in added baggage consisting of assorted bottles of excellent wine, jars of farm-made jellies and jams, great gifts for the folks back home and a couple of samples of "meat pies" for later.

145

SUNNYBROOK FARM WINERY

**Summer
Peach**

Peach Wine/Vin de Pêche

11% alc./vol.   750 ml

SERVE CHILLED • SERVIR FRAIS
PRODUCT OF CANADA • PRODUIT DU CANADA
SUNNYBROOK FARM ESTATE WINERY, NIAGARA-ON-THE-LAKE, ONTARIO

Sunnybrook Farm Estate Winery

LOCATION:	1425 Lakeshore Road, R.R. #3
	Niagara-on-the-Lake, Ontario L0S 1J0
	(905) 468-1122
HOURS:	10 AM to 6 PM, Mon.-Sat.
	1 PM to 5 PM, Sundays
	Closed Mon. & Tues. in winter
AMENITIES:	Tasting room

Yes, there is a Rebecca of Sunnybrook Farm and she is the daughter of Gerald and Vivien Goertz, proprietors of Ontario's only exclusive fruit (non-grape) winery. The Goertz family entered the winery business as "a matter of necessity" according to Gerald Goertz. "Fruit farming just wasn't making its own way, plus in 1992 we received some late hail that bruised the fruit and forced us to dump tons of product. After that we looked for alternative fruit by-products. We decided that there were too many people making jams, jellies and fruit juices so we turned to my old hobby of making wine to see if we could make a living at it."

The Goertz family is a perfect example of how a farmer who has fallen on hard times can help himself out of trouble with a little ingenuity and hard work. And the future looks bright. Sunnybrook Farm Winery has won widespread recognition for its peach, pear, apple and cherry wines and it has sold almost everything it has produced since its modest beginning in 1993.

Sunnybrook Farm does not grow grapes, so tree fruit is relied on exclusively to support the winery. With over 30 years of fruit farming experience, Goertz doesn't worry about the quality of the raw product he works with. Nor does he have a problem with the finished product. The wines all project a fresh fruit flavor and delicate taste that is extremely attractive. Though some of the wines may contain a higher degree of sweetness on the Ontario sugar chart, they are neither cloying nor syrupy.

Fruit wines are usually better for basting, marinating or as a simple refreshing drink, but many of the Sunnybrook Farm wines could easily be matched with foods like chicken or ham and would make excellent companions for a picnic barbecue.

Yes, there really is a Rebecca of Sunnybrook Farm and she has grown up to be a fine, well-adjusted young lady who helps her folks on the farm.

Thirty Bench Winery

LOCATION: 4281 Mountain View Road
(South of Highway 8)
Beamsville, Ontario
(905) 388-6271

HOURS: 10 AM to 5 PM, Weekends

AMENITIES: Tasting & retail room

THIRTY BENCH

RIESLING
ICE WINE
1992

Grown, Produced and Bottled by Commonty
Vineyard and Winery, Beamsville, Ontario

11% alc./vol.   375 ml

Product of Canada / Produit du Canada

Thirty Bench Winery is a new winery, although its owner is not new to Ontario's wine scene. Dr. Thomas Muckle is a medical doctor, but his love for home winemaking led him to be one of the founders of Cave Spring Cellars. That winery became very successful...a little too successful, and too fast for Muckle's purposes. Muckle sold his interest in the winery and began the long tedious legal process of establishing another, but smaller, winery.

A few years ago Muckle and his group of investors purchased a thirty-acre plot of land on the Beamsville bench (a flat, raised area of land between Lake Ontario's shoreline and its backdrop escarpment). The soil of the bench, deposited from Ice Age glaciers, combined with its insulated micro-climate, produces grapes that give its wine more body and a distinctive flavor. Riesling grows very well in the region and thrives on the Beamsville bench. Thirty Bench Winery is developing Cabernet Franc and Cabernet Sauvignon in the vineyard as well. They also purchase Chardonnay from a nearby neighbor.

Thirty Bench Winery gets its name from the Thirty Mile Creek that runs through the area. The names of the creeks, according to Muckle's story, were created by an early governor's wife who took a fancy to canoeing along the areas creeks. As she would progress northwest away from Niagara Falls toward Hamilton, she would name the creeks as mile markers. Hence, Twenty Mile Creek was twenty miles from the Falls and so on. Muckle maintains the good lady must of become a bit weary as she ventured on. The further she went, the shorter the differences became. There are indeed ten miles between Twenty and Thirty Mile Creeks, but only five miles between Thirty and Forty Mile Creeks. No one seemed to take exception, however, and the creeks became commercial waterways and have given birth to towns with churches, schools and inns along their shores. And as of the summer of 1995, there is even a winery along the Thirty Mile...and one to watch for small batches of hand-crafted wines.

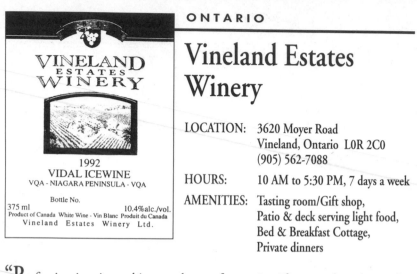

Vineland Estates Winery

LOCATION:	3620 Moyer Road Vineland, Ontario L0R 2C0 (905) 562-7088
HOURS:	10 AM to 5:30 PM, 7 days a week
AMENITIES:	Tasting room/Gift shop, Patio & deck serving light food, Bed & Breakfast Cottage, Private dinners

"Perfection in winemaking results not from scientific procedure, but rather an artistic expression upon a most natural canvas of sun, soil and fruit, coupled with the catalyst of time." When a winery shows this kind of empathy toward its work, you know you are assured a special experience when you visit the premises and encounter the wines.

The Vineland Estates property dates back to the mid-1800's and is considered one of the most picturesque winery settings in Ontario. A large deck and covered patio provides a panoramic view of the vineyards that is an enticing invitation to partake in Vineland's hospitality with light menu fare and a fine selection of well-crafted wines.

The scene is so stimulating that it is likely you may find yourself wishing you didn't have to leave. This is made possible by renting the charming Bed & Breakfast Cottage on the grounds. It is fully equipped and sleeps four. You may have to curtail your imagination for another time, however, since reservations for the engaging Cottage are reserved well in advance.

Another popular building on the property is the completely restored Carriage House which originally housed the horses and carriages of the early settlers. The quaint stone-walled facility is a busy center for weddings, private dinners and wine tastings, art exhibits and any number of group or family functions.

The 50 acre vineyards of Vineland Estates are planted with a combination of Vinifera and French hybrid grape varieties including a heavy planting of Riesling used in the making of four different wine styles. Most notable is the Riesling Icewine. Vineland is one of the few Ontario makers of the specialty wine using the Germanic grape variety. The winery is also in an expansion mode that includes a ten acre block of Merlot and a small experimental planting of the grape variety Viognier.

Vinoteca Winery
Maplegrove Estate

LOCATION: 61 Caster Ave.
            Woodbridge, Ontario L4L 5Z2
            (905) 856-5700

            Maplegrove Vinoteca Estate
            4063 North Service Rd
            Beamsville, Ontario
            (905) 562-7415

HOURS: 9 AM to 6 PM, Mon.- Sat.
            Maplegrove open weekends only

AMENITIES: Tours and tasting

Giovanni Follegot arrived in Ontario from Italy in the early 1970's. His intention from the beginning was to open a winery, but restrictive legal policies forced him to wait 12 years to realize his dream. While he waited, he made good use of his time by importing and selling winemaking equipment, establishing business contacts and developing expertise in the wine trade.

Follegot finally received his winery license and built his well-equipped facility in Woodbridge, north of Toronto. His purpose in selecting that location was to appeal to the large Italian segment of Toronto's population, but he first had the difficult task of proving to the doubting Italians that good wine could be made in Canada.

Since the area's climate is not conducive to premium grape-growing the Vinoteca Winery purchased grapes from growers on the Niagara Peninsula. Follegot adopted the wine style of full fruit-flavored wines from his native Veneto region of northeast Italy where his farming family has made wine for many years. In Italy, winemaking was only part of farming for the small producers, it wasn't until the late 1950's that large numbers of Italian growers began specializing in winemaking. For Follegot it was his main objective and he succeeded in winning over his reluctant customers with determination and hard work, plus some pretty good wine. It was at this stage of Vinoteca's growth that Maplegrove Estate vineyards were established.

Today, the wineries of Vinoteca Inc. produce two styles of wine. One uses 100% Ontario grapes from Beamsville and Niagara and the other incorporates imported juice from Italy to produce very popular blended wines. The wines of Vinoteca and Maplegrove Estate are available for your enjoyment at both locations.

149

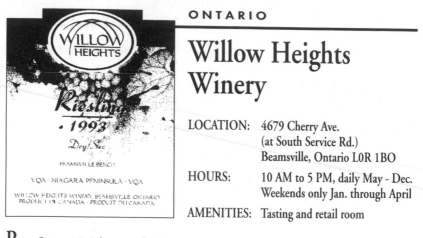

Willow Heights Winery

LOCATION: 4679 Cherry Ave.
(at South Service Rd.)
Beamsville, Ontario L0R 1B0

HOURS: 10 AM to 5 PM, daily May - Dec.
Weekends only Jan. through April

AMENITIES: Tasting and retail room

Ron Speranzini has worked 25 years as a quality assurance manager for a local steel company. For the past 15 years he has also distinguished himself as an accomplished amateur winemaker. His expertise became so apparent that many of his colleagues and friends in the industry convinced him to utilize his talent commercially. In 1992, Speranzini purchased a ten-acre farm containing established Chardonnay and Seyval Blanc vines. The original location of the winery was set in a willow grove so Speranzini commissioned a local craftsman to design and build the retail room furniture and tasting bar out of willow trees. The theme was carried over to artwork that decorates the winery and the labels of the Willow Heights wines. Work was being completed on the winery while he waited to be approved for a winery retail license. Two years later, in December of 1994, Speranzini opened the doors of his small winery and began a new chapter in Ontario's wine lore.

Speranzini explains his entry into the winery business as "a passion to be part of the wine industry." His passion is not without talent, either. With his first release of wines in the spring of 1995, Speranzini won four awards, including "Best of Show" for his 1992 Reserve Chardonnay at the 1995 Cuveé, a three-day showcase of Ontario wines held each year in Niagara Falls.

Willow Heights offers excellent examples of Chardonnay, Pinot Noir and Icewine to visitors. A Seyval Blanc will also be released in 1995 and Speranzini has already entered into contracts with local growers to produce Zinfandel and Syrah grapes. He hopes to be the first winery in Ontario to release wines made from these varieties.

The future looks promising for the Willow Heights Winery. As its enthusiastic winemaker says, "there's plenty of room in the marketplace for good quality wine." And we might add that it can be found in the tasting room of this small, but "soon to be famous" winery.

PENNSYLVANIA

The picturesque village of North East lies near the shore of Lake Erie in the heart of the Lake Erie Wine Region of Pennsylvania. Ninety-six percent of the grapes grown in the state are from this concentrated area that boasts a growing season of over 190 days and includes over 15,000 acres of grapes in Erie County alone. Five wineries make up Northwest Pennsylvania's portion of a vast and productive wine district which is one of the largest viticultural regions in North America spanning a total of 40,000 acres in three states.

The cool spring and summer lake breezes plus the plateau-like topography of the shoreline blend their natural forces to create ideal growing conditions for classic, native and hybrid grape varieties.

Pennsylvania's grape-growing industry dates back to the early 1800's and has been a consistent producer of native American, French hybrid and more recently, European vinifera varieties. Welsh's, with their popular grape juice products, are universally credited for propagating grape-growing in the Lake Erie Wine Region. Concord, Catawba, Niagara and Delaware were the primary grapes of choice for juice producers. As times and tastes changed, growers began experimenting with hybrid wine grape varieties such as Vidal, Seyval and Vignoles. Today, a new generation of wine growers is attracting attention with the successful development of Riesling, Chardonnay and Cabernet Franc vineyards.

With Pennsylvania's passage of the 1968 Limited Winery Act, growers were allowed the opportunity to build wineries and make wine from the fruit they grew. Also allowed in the Act was the ability to establish winery retail tasting rooms, so long as 100% Pennsylvania-grown fruit was used in the production of the wine. The wines are also available at winery retail outlets in larger cities like Philadelphia and Pittsburgh as well as some limited availability in state liquor stores and restaurants.

The wine industry continues to grow in Pennsylvania and the wines improve with each succeeding harvest. Improved technology, tourism and research have all contributed to make the state's wine industry a viable investment, but the dedication of old and new farming families is the backbone of what makes the wine industry and agriculture in general thrive in Pennsylvania.

Conneaut Cellars Winery

LOCATION: P.O. Box 5075
Route 322
(Exit 36-B off I-79)
Conneaut Lake, PA 16316

HOURS: 10 AM to 6 PM, daily
Closed Mondays, Jan. to March

AMENITIES: Tasting room, Picnic area, Gift shop

There are not many winemakers with a Ph.D. in psychology, or who have retired from a career in the State Department. Alan Wolf of Conneaut Cellars fits both classifications. Why winemaking, you may ask? "Its pretty simple," states Wolf, "I was exposed to and learned winemaking while I was with the State Department in Germany. We used to place border-crossing political refugees as workers in wineries until such time as we could get them into the States. I got pretty interested in the winery business and decided I would open a winery when I retired."

With the influence of German winemaking, one would expect that Wolf's Conneaut Cellars wines would have the same characteristics. "Not so," says Wolf, "I learned what not to do and developed our own style." That style is one that has created wines with some unusual names like "Princess Snowater," "Iroquois Gold" or "Finn Ditch Red." "We use proprietary names so people don't pre-judge our wines before they taste them," explains Wolf. He has definitely achieved that objective. It is tough to venture a guess as to what kind of wine "Huidekoper" or "Wolf Island" will be, but then isn't that the fun of drinking wine? Isn't that why wines are presented at competitions without labels? No preconceived judgments until the wine is tasted and evaluated for what it is, on its own merits.

Conneaut Cellars contracts all its grapes from the Lake Erie Region of Pennsylvania and produces wines from a broad spectrum of French hybrid, vinifera and native American grapes. Conneaut's Cabernet Sauvignon (one of the few wines identified by a varietal name) is a noteworthy award-winner. The tasting room wine list does identify the degree of sweetness of each wine with a 0-4 scale which is helpful for visitors to match the wines with individual taste preferences. The list is also a little more descriptive of the wine style than the Wolf's fanciful names would imply.

Heritage Wine Cellars

LOCATION: 12162 East Main Rd. (Rte 20)
North East, PA 16428
(814) 725-8015

HOURS: 9 AM to 6 PM, Mon-Thurs.
9 AM to 7 PM, Fri. & Sat.
Sunday 10 AM to 6 PM
Winter hours may vary

AMENITIES: Tasting room, Custom labels

In 1833 Harvey Hall purchased the original 100 acre fruit farm that later became known as the Heritage Wine Cellars. His great-grandson, Kenneth Bostwick, converted the farm to grape production. Today, great-great-grandson Robert manages several farms totaling nearly 400 acres of vineyards.

Heritage Wine Cellars is located in a restored 18th century barn, nestled in the heart of the Lake Erie Wine Region. The black walnut wood framework is an impressive piece of farm architecture supported by 60 and 70 foot beams throughout the structure. Just walking into the hospitality room of the old barn, one gets a nostalgic feeling of a bygone era and a tradition that this family will not let die.

Heritage Wine Cellars offer an ample assortment of wines from locally grown Pennsylvania grapes. From the sweet, grapy Concord to the unique and distinctive Isabella, to the crisp, yet delicate Seyval Blanc, there is a match for each individual taste.

In the tasting room you'll also find "Homemade Heritage Jellies" to augment your selection of wine. The winemaker's family has taken some of the grape varieties used in the wine production to make an assortment of jellies to delight tastebuds and add an extra taste sensation to favorite foods. A variety of nicely packaged wine and jelly gift packs are available.

A major part of the winery's business is devoted to custom wine labeling of bottles. From wedding and party favors to special occasions and holiday gifts the computer age has made it possible to have an individually personalized label for your wine purchase.

A visit to the Heritage Wine Cellars is a pleasing trip back in time and a sharing of a farm family's traditions. In fact, most days you'll find Grandpa Bostwick in the tasting room ready and willing to share stories of the old days of farming in the Lake Erie Region while you sample the tasty fruits of his family's effort.

Mazza Vineyards

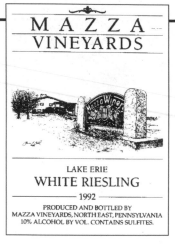

LAKE ERIE
WHITE RIESLING
1992
PRODUCED AND BOTTLED BY
MAZZA VINEYARDS, NORTH EAST, PENNSYLVANIA
10% ALCOHOL BY VOL. CONTAINS SULFITES.

LOCATION: 11815 East Lake Rd (Rte 5)
North East, PA 16428
(814) 725-8695

HOURS: 9 AM to 8 PM, Mon-Sat.
July and August
9 AM to 5:30 PM, Mon-Sat.
Sept. through June
Sun. 11AM to 4:30 PM, Year round

AMENITIES: Tasting room, Picnic pavilion,
Labor Day Weekend festival,
Various festival events

Robert Mazza was born in Italy where his family operated a farm with grapes, chestnuts, figs, prickly pears and a various assortment of other food products. As a child Mazza came to the United States and eventually earned a degree in engineering. As a young man, Mazza and his brother expanded an interest in home winemaking to a full-fledged commercial business.

Having an interest in home winemaking and limited experience in grape growing is a far cry from being a winemaker, so the Mazzas' sought the best professional help they could find for their modest venture in 1973. They found a German enologist who had just graduated top of his class at the famed German wine college, Geisenheim. After five years of setting up the wine making operation and training Mazza's current winemaker, Gary Mosier, the young German winemaker returned to his Fatherland and has since become the administrator of the famous von Zimmer Winery in the Rheingau.

Mazza Vineyards contracts all the grapes for their wine from local growers and the scenic drive to the handsome Mediterranean-design winery along East Lake Road leads through mile after mile of rows of French hybrid, vinifera and native American vines. Even though Mazza does not grow the grapes, winery personnel are very much involved in the care and development of the vineyards and set high standards of production from the growers to meet the quality demands of the winemaker.

Robert Mazza is so dedicated to the concept of high quality wines that he has helped organized the recently-formed Lake Erie Quality Wine Alliance. This organization of wineries spans 40,000 acres of vineyards in three states. As the Alliance's first president, Mazza is beginning to write the newest chapter in the 150-year tradition of grape-growing and winemaking on the Lake Erie shores of northern Ohio, northeastern Pennsylvania and western New York.

Penn Shore Winery and Vineyards

LOCATION: 10225 East Lake Rd (Rte 5)
North East, PA 16428
(814) 725-8688

HOURS: 9 AM to 8 PM, Mon-Sat.
July and August
9 AM to 5:30 PM, Mon-Sat.
Sept. through June
Sun. 11AM to 5 PM
Year round

AMENITIES: Tasting room

Just down the road from Mazza Vineyards and a few minutes' drive from I-90 is the Penn Shore Winery and Vineyards. Mazza has controlling interest in this winery property that was established by three area grape growers. The three original founders of Penn Shore, George Luke, Blair McCord and George Sceiford, were instrumental in the passage of the Pennsylvania Limited Winery Act of 1968. This piece of state legislation allowed grape growers the opportunity of developing wineries and selling their wine to the public directly from winery tasting rooms. Only wine products from Pennsylvania-grown fruit are permitted under this license, however, and the law does not allow for the distribution and sale of these wines in general retail stores.

In 1988, Robert Mazza brought his management expertise to Penn Shore and the property has continued to prosper. Penn Shore's stable of wines feature primarily products under $7. Their premium vintage wines consist of French Hybrid Seyval, Vidal Blanc and Vignoles, also known as Ravat. The Vignoles is also available in a sweet Late Harvest version that the winery proudly states has won a Gold Medal in competition. Penn Shore produces an oak-aged Chardonnay for around $9 that is popular with tasting room visitors.

In the volume "jug style" table wines, Penn Shore offers the native American grape varieties of Concord, Niagara and Catawba to customers who wish to remain loyal to the grapes that are indigenous to this cool Lake Erie Region. These *Labrusca* grape varieties are presented in both their individual style and in a series of blended specialty wines consisting of varying degrees of sweetness and fruitiness.

The helpful staff of Penn Shore will cordially guide you through the entire winemaking process and provide a delightful tasting of their wines.

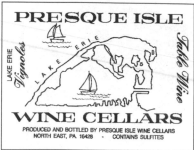

Presque Isle Wine Cellars

LOCATION: 9440 Buffalo Rd (Rte 20)
                   North East, PA 16428
                   (814) 725-1314

HOURS: 8 AM to 5 PM, Mon-Sat.
                   Open Sun. during harvest

AMENITIES: Tasting room,
                   Complete winemaking supplies

If you have ever contemplated or are currently making wine at home, then Presque Isle Wine Cellars is a must place for you to visit, or at the very least, obtain their *Winemaking Supply Catalogue*. Doug and Marlene Moorhead have been supplying the **complete** needs of amateur and professional winemakers for over 30 years. Presque Isle, which is a misspelling of the French word *presquile* meaning peninsula, has become the main source of supplies and expert guidance for home winemakers from all over the U.S. and Canada.

The Moorheads have grown grapes in the area for three generations and currently tend 160 acres with the majority of the vineyards planted with Concord and Niagara juice grapes which are sold to Welsh's Juice Co. About 30 acres are devoted to wine grapes from which they make wine under the Presque Isle Wine Cellars label that is sold only at the tasting room. Presque Isle produces and sells over 25,000 gallons of fresh juice to home winemakers every fall. It's a very big part of their business, so much so that when most wineries cut back their public hours due to the hectic pace of the harvest season, Presque Isle expands theirs to accommodate supplying fresh juice to eager winemakers.

The wine grapes of the Presque Isle vineyards are primarily *vinifera* (Chardonnay, Pinot Noir, Riesling, Cabernet Sauvignon and Cabernet Franc) and French hybrid (Foch, Seyval, Chambourcin and Vidal). Presque Isle offers a selection of juice from 20-25 grape varieties each fall. Judging from the orders they receive each year from their *Grape and Juice Prospectus*, the quality is top notch and in much demand.

Although over 90% of Presque Isle's business is as a mail order supplier to amateur winemakers and small commercial wineries, there is still the opportunity for the general consumer to visit the winery tasting room and sample the fine wines they personally make and purchase some real gems to take home.

WISCONSIN

Kewaunee and Door Counties in northeastern Wisconsin form that familiar peninsula on the map that begins at the city of Green Bay and extends about 70 miles into Lake Michigan. The area's climate, soil and growing conditions are ideal for fruit growing, especially cherries and apples. Due to its westerly location in the Great Lakes region, however, the warming effects of Lake Michigan winds are not as extensive as on the eastern border and therefore the area experiences a somewhat cooler fall. Grapes, which need a slightly longer growing season than tree fruit, are more difficult to grow in this cooler temperate zone than in other parts of the Great Lakes. As a result, fruit wines have become the specialty of the area. Those grape wines that are offered by peninsula wineries are made from grapes imported from either central or southern Wisconsin, Michigan or the West Coast of the U.S.

The wineries of the peninsula, Door Peninsula, Orchard Country and von Stiehl have made the most out of the situation by establishing three successful winery/retail operations with a production based in fruit wines. Since the area is a very popular visitors attraction, all three wineries have geared their products and merchandising techniques to the tourist trade which also generates return sales via mail orders.

This picturesque Wisconsin peninsula is well-established in the tradition and reputation of the great Dairy State with an abundance of dairy farms and corn fields prominent throughout the countryside, but the area north of Sturgeon Bay is dominated by thousands of acres of bountiful fruit orchards. During the summer and harvest festival seasons, Highways 42 and 57 are busy with sightseeing motorists going to and fro. It is best to base day excursions out of either Green Bay or Sturgeon Bay, or make reservations well in advance for the scattering of "Mom & Pop" motel operations. By all means, indulge in Door County's fish boils that are offered at almost every eatery in each little town. Fish boils run about $12-$15 and include beverage and dessert (usually fresh cherry pie).

The fruit wines of Wisconsin are in a special wine classification, as are all fruit wines. They are full-flavored, well-made and although their fruity sweetness may not serve as well for dinner wines as do Great Lakes grape-based table wines, they have certainly built a successful niche for themselves as cooking and basting wines, dessert wines and as increasingly popular refreshing "cooler" wines for casual consumption. The growers and winemakers of this fruitful Great Lakes peninsula take pride in their production of quality fruit wines and they are rewarded for their efforts each year by tens of thousands of visitors and patrons to their hospitality rooms.

Door Peninsula Winery

DOOR COUNTY

Sweet Cherry Wine

A Natural Sweet Wine From
Door County Cherries

ALCOHOL 10%
BY VOLUME

CONTAINS
SULFITES

LOCATION:	5806 Highway 42 North (8 miles north of Sturgeon Bay) Sturgeon Bay, WI 54235 (414) 743-7431
HOURS:	9 AM -6 PM, 7 days a week Open year round
AMENITIES:	Hospitality room, Guided tours, Gifts & mail orders

It is best stated in the Door Peninsula Winery brochure, "Door County's picturesque and historic fruit-producing habitat provides an appropriate setting for the Door Peninsula Winery. Orchards from the area produce an abundance of succulent fruit used in making the winery's highly regarded fruit wines."

"The harvest begins in July with the ripening of the red tart Montmorency cherries. This is followed by the fall harvest of plums, pears, and apples which in turn are pressed into juice and transported to the winery where the winemaker begins the fermentation process which changes the juice into Door Peninsula Winery's award-winning premium fruit wines."

As you enjoy your drive up Highway 42, the billboards announcing the winery do not adequately prepare you for the unusual setting of a nineteenth century schoolhouse housing the winery. In 1974 the schoolhouse was renovated and the Door Peninsula Winery established its operations in the building. Visitors will find that the winery has retained the charm of the old country school with an attractive and friendly decor which makes the winery tour an interesting and for many, a nostalgic experience.

As you are guided through the Door Peninsula Winery's cool darkened wine cellar you will see wines in various stages of fermentation and aging. Next is a vivid and thorough video presentation explaining the entire winemaking process. The winery tour lasts about twenty minutes and concludes in the tasting salon where you may sample and buy the complete line of Door Peninsula fruit wines plus a variety of other food products including gourmet mustards, sauces, candies, wine jellies and even a cherry wine cheddar cheese spread.

The Door Peninsula Winery is a very busy place from summer through Green Bay Packers football season, but it's worth the time and effort, if only to bring home bottles of their popular Christmas Wines. These specialty items, from a blend of cherry and grape wine to mulled cherry wine, are admittedly novelty wines for the tourist, but they do offer an unusual choice of flavors that have their own unique appeal and...you won't find them anywhere else.

Orchard Country Winery

ORCHARD COUNTRY WINERY

DOOR COUNTY
SWEET CHERRY WINE
ALCOHOL 11% BY VOLUME
CONTAINS SULFITES
Cellared & Bottled by Orchard Country Winery, Fish Creek, WI 54212

Store in a Cool Place
Refrigerate After Opening

LOCATION: 9197 Highway 42
Fish Creek, WI 54212
(414) 868-3479

HOURS: 9 AM to 5 PM, daily
May through October
Open weekends through
the winter months

AMENITIES: Free tastings, Winery & orchard tours,
Orchard market, Gifts & Antiques

Orchard Country Winery lives up to its name. This most northern winery on the Door Peninsula is surrounded by acres of bountiful apple and cherry orchards, but no vineyards. When you visit the Orchard Country Winery you are in the heart of the Door Peninsula's "orchard country" and there's no mistaking the agriculture of this area.

In the mid-1980's processed fruit was too bountiful, prices fell and demand did not pick up the slack. The Lautenbach family had to come up with a solution to utilize their crops. They recognized that the area was growing as a tourist area due to the beautiful beaches and large state parks, so they decided to make their own products from the fruit of their hundred-acre orchard and sell them from a farm market. Business has been brisk ever since.

An old restored dairy barn serves as home for the Orchard Country Winery located at the back of the parking area of the Orchard Market. The market features fresh fruit, fresh-pressed cider, a variety of Door County's home-made products and fruit-country related gifts. Here visitors can enjoy sampling various fruit wines (cherry, apple, plum and raspberry) and ciders (apple, cherry and apple/cherry) or gather around a video showing the harvesting of cherries. During the harvest season, visitors can actually witness mechanical harvesters gathering the current crop from a tractor-pulled tour wagon.

In the spring of the year, Orchard Country features horse-drawn tours through the beauty of the fruit blossoms, and in the winter, sleigh rides create a romantic setting among the snow-covered trees.

Door County may not be a mecca for the consummate wine connoisseur, but the countryside is scenic, the people are friendly and there are some very tasty fruit products to please the entire family.

von Stiehl Winery

LOCATION: 115 Navarino Street
Algoma, WI 54201
(414) 487-5208

HOURS: 9 AM to 5 PM, Daily
May through December
11 to 4 PM, Jan. - April

AMENITIES: Guided Tours (May-Oct.) with
video presentation, Free Tasting,
Gift Haus

Cherry wine is king on the Door County Peninsula and the von Stiehl Winery has made the most of a good thing by pleasing customers and winning awards for their peninsula cherry wine since 1964. The von Stiehl Winery is the oldest continuous winery in the state of Wisconsin and is situated in a former brewery built in 1868 in the quaint little town of Algoma just a thirty minute drive east of Green Bay and a few miles south of the Door County line.

In the early years of the winery, Charles Stiehl, a medical doctor, hand-wrapped his precious bottles of cherry and apple wine with protective gauze and encased it with a plaster of paris mixture. This patented process was created to protect the wine from sunlight and changing temperatures. The "bottle cast" is still used on a limited number of bottles of the winery's signature cherry wine and is a very popular item in the wine sales room.

You can't help but notice some strange-looking characters throughout the winery overlooking visitors and the entire winemaking process. They are the von Stiehl trolls that "make sure only the good spirits stay in the wine." A whole collection of von Stiehl mascot trolls are on display and are for sale in the winery's tasting room.

The von Stiehl winery produces primarily fruit wines (cherries, apples and pears) grown a few miles up the peninsula. Grape wines are also made from grapes grown in southern Wisconsin and in the Lake Michigan Shore region of Michigan. The growing season on the peninsula is too short for most varieties of wine grapes, however, owner/winemaker Bill Schmiling is still experimenting with hybrids in the hope of developing a reliable variety conducive to the area.

All told, the von Stiehl winery offers twenty-two styles of wine (mostly fruit wines of varying degrees of sweetness), an interesting tour of the historic winery that offers some unique facets to winemaking not seen elsewhere and an extensive "Gift Haus" that will please even the most discriminating shopper.

The Most Frequently Asked Questions About Wine and...

WINEMAKING

Q: What determines when the wine process is complete at the winery and the finished product is ready to be released to the public?

A: Making wine is not just an art. It is also a science requiring precise procedures and controls, combined with personal judgment and assessment based on hundreds of sensory experiences and evaluations. Whether or not a wine is "ready" for bottling or release to the public is a matter of judgment. Scientific procedures and equipment can assist the vintner in making the wine and aging it properly, but the day comes when the winemaker must rely on the basic senses of sight, taste and smell. Drawing on his or her knowledge and years of experience, the vintner pronounces the wine ready to leave the winery and be welcomed, opened and enjoyed on the tables of wine drinkers everywhere.

Q: I've seen the reference to "yeast" a number of times when reading about winemaking. What part does yeast play in the process?

A: The English word "yeast" comes from either the Greek "zestos" or Sanskrit "yasyati," both meaning to "boil" without heat, referring to a yeast-induced fermentation. Next to the grape, yeast is the most important element in wine, for this microscopic plant organism is the sole producer of fermentation that changes grape juice into wine. Yeasts "eat" or metabolize the natural sugars in the grapes and produce, in equal amounts, alcohol and an inert gas called carbon dioxide that accounts for the bubbles in sparkling wines like champagne. Although "wild" yeasts occur naturally on grapes, they are sometimes unpredictable in winemaking. Over the years, researchers have isolated a number of "cultured" strains in a pure form that offer subtle flavor nuances and other desirable attributes to the finished wine.

Q: How does barrel aging come into play with the development of premium wines?

A: Wines meant for continued aging (such as Cabernet Sauvignon, Pinot

Noir, Chancellor and Chardonnay) are immature, rough and reflect the simple fruit of the grape when taken from the fermenting tanks. The transformation of a young wine to a mature, complex one starts in the barrel and is completed through bottle aging. During oak aging, the sharp, fruity, fermented wine softens into more appealing and refined flavors. The barrel allows a slow penetration of air in the wine, permitting aging to occur. At the same time, it imparts a small amount of oak character which marries with the wine and adds complexity. The traditional 60 gallon oak barrel is the optimum size for balancing wine aging, through air penetration, and the oak character acquired by the wine. A larger barrel or tank lacks sufficient wine/wood contact while a smaller barrel may contribute too much oak before the wine has had adequate time to mature.

Q: With the success of French/American hybrid wine grapes in the Great Lakes, I wonder if it was the French or the Americans who developed the vines?

A: After the plant louse phylloxera epidemic in Europe a century ago a number of France's leading biologists began breeding hybrid vines by marrying the European classics to phylloxera-resistant American species. Once they mastered the technique of grafting French originals on to American roots, and thereby solving the dreaded insect problem, they abandoned further development of hybrids. The hybrids were found to be hardy, disease resistant, productive and the wines made from them were of excellent quality. Because of these attributes, the vines were much more suitable to the growing conditions of eastern North America than were most of the European varieties. Further research and development of the hybrid varieties was conducted at the Geneva Agricultural Station in New York State. Many of the hybrid varietals are also very popular in the new vineyards of England and New Zealand.

Q: Would you please tell me which of the following French hybrid grape varieties are used for white wine: Seyval, Chancellor, Vidal, Vignoles, De Chaunac and Foch?

A: Seyval (say-voll), Vidal (vee-doll), and Vignoles (vin-yole) are the three primary French hybrid grapes used to make white wines from very dry to semi-sweet. Chancellor and Foch (foe-shh) are premium red grapes. De Chaunac (day-shawn-uc) is a red grape that also makes an excellent "blush" wine as well as a red table wine.

Q: About fifteen years ago I made some grape wine. It has been sitting down in my basement all that time and I wonder if it is any good to drink?

A: It is quite possible that the wine is just fine. There is only one way to find out and that is to open it up. Your nose will be the first indication as to whether you wish to taste it or not. If it smells bad, it will more than likely taste the same way. It would be kind of fun just to see how well you did fifteen years ago.

Q: What do wineries mean when they say they "rack" the wine?

A: "Racking" is the movement of a wine from one container to another. This is a natural and traditional method of wine clarification by which precipitated solids are left behind with each movement of the wine. These solids are the natural residual deposits of the winemaking process and it continues sometimes in the bottle. This is why it is often recommended to decant an older wine into a clean, clear decanter before serving it to your guests. These deposits are in no way harmful, but they do taste bitter.

Q: While taking a tour through a winery the guide said that workers enter the large wine tanks from a small hole on the bottom to clean it out. Was he kidding? How can an adult get through an opening no bigger than eighteen or twenty inches?

A: When wine is moved from one tank to another it will leave small particles of grape solids, skins and yeast that have settled on the bottom and sides of the tank. It is necessary to sanitize the inside of these tanks and barrels before new wine can be placed in them. Although with the use of pressure and suction hoses most of the residual can be removed, the final step necessitates the placement of someone into the tank to insure cleanliness with an inspection. There is a trick to it. It is done by first placing the arms over the head. You then insert one shoulder, followed by the other, at which point you push yourself through. Using the proper technique, even quite a large person can enter a tank without great difficulty.

Q: I was part of a large group that toured a winery and the tour guide said wine is taken out of the storage barrels by wine thieves. I was unable to ask the question, but what is a "wine thief"? It isn't what it suggests is it?

A: It isn't a masked bandit, if that's what you mean. But it is a device to "steal" the wine from the barrel for testing. A wine thief is a simple hollow tube, usually made of glass or stainless steel, that is inserted through the bung hole of a barrel to withdraw a sample of the wine. This is a daily process for the winemaker in determining when the wine is ready to bottle or for extracting samples for one of the many laboratory analyses that are constantly being conducted at the winery.

Q: What effect do corks have on wine? Once a cork is pulled from a wine bottle, what should I look for?

A: The cork is an organic closure which permits the interchange of air with the wine at a rate that allows the wine to mature. Wine bottles with corks should be stored either upside down or on their sides, so the cork remains moist and does not dry out. A simple squeeze of the cork will give a clue as what to expect in the wine. If it is hard and dry, or crumbly from the corkscrew, the wine may have been stored improperly and it may be a sign of poor quality. If the cork is soft and moist, but not mushy, it's an indication of proper storage. Mold on the top of a cork in the bottle is not necessarily a bad sign. Just wipe off the lip and taste the wine for the true test.

Q: If a wine cork that has gone bad for one reason or another imparts an unpalatable taste to the wine, then why even use a cork in the first place?

A: Cork is used as a wine closure because it is a natural product, from the bark of a cork oak tree, that has elastic properties that enable it to conform to irregularities in the neck of a bottle for a better seal. Also, there are some schools of thought that believe cork aids in the development of a wine aging in a bottle by imparting a minute amount of cork flavor. The intensity of this flavor naturally increases the longer the wine is in the bottle. It is almost imperceptible in the first few years of aging, as it is developed very slowly. This is based on the assumption that the cork and the wine are in constant contact. The alcohol in the wine slowly extracts the flavor from the cork. These are the reasons why a cork is the traditional closure. It was thought, until recently questioned by the scientists at the University of California at Davis, that air was transmitted through the cork to the wine enhancing its ability to age. With elaborate testing results, these scientists refute this theory. Research never ends in the wine industry.

Q: Before corks were discovered, what was used to seal the wine from the air?

A: A layer of olive oil was commonly used to seal the mouth of the clay storage jar called amphora. This technique was used for centuries before the invention of both the cork and the bottle, which happened around the same time.

Q: I remember as a child helping my grandfather pick and crush grapes to make wine. Today everything looks to be highly mechanized. Is wine made in the old traditional way by hand any more?

A: Almost all of the small wineries in the world still rely on manual labor to harvest their crops, only the very large operations find it economical to invest in mechanical pickers and other labor saving machines. Although the practice of "grape stomping" is virtually extinct, it is still practiced for show at festivals and for the tourists at wineries. Even with the modernization of equipment not much had changed in the process of making wine for centuries, until the last few decades. Today, even the old-timers are paying attention to scientific research on the growing of vines, the intricacies of natural chemistry involved with winemaking and various techniques available to increase the quality of production. A scientific approach to agriculture is more the rule in most wine growing regions around the world with guesswork and chance being reduced. Until someone learns how to control Mother Nature, however, grape-growing and winemaking will still be the ultimate product of land, weather and hard hands-on work.

Q: What happens if a winery or farmer plants a particular variety of grapevine and after the four or five years it takes to mature, the variety is out of favor with the consumer?

A: You have probably already guessed the obvious answer. They must pull up the vineyard and replant it or let it go wild on its own. It is extremely costly to tear out and replant vineyards, so much care and research goes into the decision of what and how much to plant. For the most part, unless a farmer took a big gamble on predicting the public's wine taste, most pull ups of vineyards are minimal. They do happen, however, on a regular basis with wineries who constantly adjust to the changing pulse of the American consumer.

Q: I met a farmer who said he grows grapes and sells them to wineries. I thought wineries grew their own grapes?

A: Not necessarily. Many of the wineries do plant vineyards for their wine, but they often need more grapes than they can grow so they buy from independent growers. Larger wineries, as a matter of regular business, contract with growers to supply all the grapes that will be needed to meet projected production needs. The winemaker works very closely with these growers to be sure they meet the standards of production they specify to achieve the quality of wine desired. Since the contracts between the winery and the grower are very specific about the type of grape, the production yield and quality control, the wineries know exactly what they will be working with, provided Mother Nature cooperates.

Q: Why do some wine labels carry the name of the grape and some have a name that seems to be "made up"?

A: When a wine is made from at least 75% of a particular grape variety it is called a "varietal" wine and the name of the grape may be used on the label. Some typical examples of varietal wines are: Cabernet Sauvignon, Chardonnay, Seyval, Vidal Blanc, Chancellor, Riesling and there are many more. The tendency of late is to blend a mixture of compatible varieties in order to give the winemaker an opportunity to use the best grapes available, and exercise some creative winemaking to produce the best possible product and value. These are called "proprietary" wines because they are a blend of wines developed by the proprietor and carry such creative private label names as Trillium, Jester's Blush, Lilac Hill or simply, White Table wine. Some people have the mistaken perception that "varietal" wines are the best quality wines. That is not always the case. Mouton Cadet, many French chateau bottled wines and most all Champagnes are just a few examples of famous blended proprietary wines of top quality.

Q: If frost in the spring and rain at harvest are the villains of the vineyards, does that mean the summer is easy going for grape growers?

A: Not by a long shot! Although uncontrollable frost and rain are more critical to the outcome of the total production, there is still the constant battle with insects and fungus diseases, such as mites and mildew. Growers have learned to control these problems with environmentally safe sprays, but nature's biggest pests to the maturing grape bunches are birds. Great clouds of birds have been know to assault a vineyard and eat it clean of grapes within a few hours. Growers have tried nets, shotguns, recorded sounds and even recordings on timers that go off with a variety of blaring sound effects to scare the birds. Nothing works effectively for long, but fortunately the bird problem is not widespread nor is it consistent from year to year. The bird situation was so bad a while back that one Michigan winemaker who had a particular grape variety completely wiped out, released a fully packaged bottle minus the wine and called the product, "The Wine The Birds Ate". Wine critics considered it "too lacking in body".

ENTERTAINING

Q: How do I go about putting together a wine-tasting party for friends?

A: Organizing a wine-tasting is relatively simple and offers a unique experience for your guests. The first thing you have to determine is the theme. For instance, "The wines of the Niagara Peninsula" or "Champagnes of the Great Lakes". The possibilities are endless and your local wine merchant will be of invaluable help in the planning. Always plan a selection of different styles of wines and serve the whites before the reds and the dry before the sweet wines. This will make it easier for your taste buds to distinguish subtle differences. Have plenty of food snacks available, but stay away from heavily seasoned or flavored foods that may overpower the wines. For those who may wish to know more about the wines, many trade associations and wineries offer booklets and materials, usually free for the asking. Be sure to have non-alcoholic drinks, such as sparkling juices for the designated drivers and plan about a total of twelve to fourteen ounces per person for the evening.

Q: How do I go about shopping for good wine values?

A: Wine is no different than anything else you shop for. Look for "specials" and featured wines that are not as well-known as the more popular and expensive alternatives. This is also an excellent opportunity to taste different types of wines inexpensively. Once you have found a few favorites, you will usually save 10 to 20 percent buying by the case. Most stores will give you a discount for mixed and multiple case purchases. Sometimes it is to your advantage to recruit a few friends and buy your wines together. It's a rather competitive industry and volume discounts, as well as individual bottle markdowns, are quite commonplace.

Q: Does keeping wine in the refrigerator harm it?

A: Actually, putting a partially full bottle in the refrigerator will help preserve the wine for a couple days until you are ready to finish it. Refrigeration slows down the natural deterioration process after the wine has been exposed to oxygen. It will not keep for much longer than a few days, however, so be sure to consume what is left within a relatively short time. Refrigeration of full bottles of wine should also be somewhat limited even though they will keep for a much longer period of time. The refrigerator is a popular hiding place for champagne, but it is not the best place for storing your collection. Months of refrigeration will have a negative effect on the quality of all wines.

Q: What is the proper procedure for setting wine glasses at the dinner table?

A: It is preferable to have a fresh, clean glass for each wine planned with a meal. The glasses should be clear stemware and capable of holding eight to ten ounces of wine. Etiquette dictates placing the wine glasses in the upper righthand portion of the place setting. The wines are poured half to two thirds full, from the first glass on the right of each guest (for the first course) to the last glass on the left (for dessert). If you do not have enough glasses for all the wines, use what you have and supply a pitcher of fresh water to rinse after each wine. There are some traditional wine glass shapes from various wine regions, but the all-purpose, 8 to 10 ounce, tulip-shaped glass works very well for all types of wines.

Q: I've recently increased my use of wine with cooking. Do you have any tips on cooking with wine that may be useful?

A: It seems that Americans have discovered only recently the joy of cooking with wine and the difference it can make in a very wide variety of foods. Many people have not tried cooking with wine because they are unsure of its use as a seasoning agent and how much is enough. It is difficult to overdo wine - the more you add, the more flavor you'll receive. It all depends upon how juicy or liquid you want the finished dish. Wine gives flavor to some dishes that would be bland or flat without it. The flavor of wine in cooking is due to the nature of the wine and not the alcohol. Most of the alcohol escapes during cooking and little, if any, is present in the finished dish. For meat dishes calling for wine, first heat the wine (do not boil). Adding cold wine tends to make meat tough, while warm wine helps tenderize it. For recipes calling for water, substitute wine, it will add enormously to the flavor and richness of the dish. For fish and chicken, use a dry or semi-dry white wine. Dry red wines have a better chemistry with heavier red meats. One thing to keep in mind is that when wine is first added to a dish it imparts little flavor. Therefore, it is best to let it cook for a few minutes before tasting. You will be astonished at the difference even 5 or 10 minutes make.

Q: Is it me or does wine not go very well with the salad course? I seem to have a real hard time enjoying wine with salads containing vinaigrette dressings. Are there other foods that may also not be compatible with wine?

A: Although drinking wine with a vinaigrette salad dressing may be undesirable, many cooks prefer vinegar made of wine. Strange as it may sound, wine vinegar does have a decidedly less harsh taste than cider varieties. Thus, it intermingles with and adds complexity rather than dominating other food flavors and smells. Wine vinegars can be found as red, white, herbed and spiced. They add a nice touch to a tasty crisp salad. Most foods go well with wine, but there are some flavors which should be worked around or toned down when wine is an important part of the meal. Included in these are curry, horseradish, hot peppers, citrus rinds, excessive fats and oils and heavy chocolate. In addition, one surprising food is asparagus. It can dull your palate, so it is better served as a separate course without wine.

Q: At a wine tasting party, in what order should red, white and sparkling wines be served? Do "blush" wines follow the reds?

A: As a general rule, serve white wines before reds and dry wines before sweet. Blush wines are served as you would rosé, in between the white and the red wines. The serving order is a matter of common sense rather than one of etiquette. Sweet wines have a tendency to overpower the taste buds which will give the sensation of bitterness to dry wines after the palate has been stimulated with sweetness. Heartier red wines have the same effect over white wines, so it only makes sense to serve in the suggested order to get the most enjoyment from the wines. Sparkling wines with their higher acid content and bubbles, have a tendency to clear and cleanse the palate so they may be served first or last with no loss in taste.

Q: I received a "hostess" gift of wine from my dinner guests, but it didn't match with the menu I had planned. Did I make a social blunder by not opening and serving the wine my friends brought?

A: The thoughtful "gift" was exactly that and is meant to be enjoyed by you at your leisure as a token of appreciation. If your friends expected to share the wine with you they should have told you ahead of time that they would like to bring the wine and asked for your recommendation to complement the menu.

Q: I have been invited to a "vertical" wine tasting and have no idea what to expect. Could you shed some light on what a "vertical" tasting is?

A: A "vertical" wine tasting is a popular and fun theme for a wine tasting party with friends who share a common interest in learning about wine. A vertical tasting highlights a single variety of wine produced by one vintner, but spanning a number of different years. For example, you might like to select an interesting Merlot from any one winery. By comparing various vintages, say 1985 through 1992, you will have the opportunity to witness the development of this particular grape variety in both aging and in the winemaker's progress in establishing his individual style for handling the variety. It is sometimes difficult to obtain older vintages unless they have been collected in wine cellars or purchased directly from the winery. It may be easier, therefore, to host a "horizontal" wine tasting. In this tasting the Merlot, or any variety you choose, is presented from the same vintage and from different wineries. With this tasting you get the opportunity to taste the difference in style from each winemaker using the same grape from the same harvest year.

IN GENERAL

Q: I really enjoy wine, but feel like I would be overwhelmed with what I have to know to become proficient. Please convince me I'm wrong.

A: If you enjoy wine and food, purchase wines regularly and desire to further your knowledge on the subject, then first observe your senses. Become aware of your likes and dislikes, just as you have done with food. Mentally record different tastes and aromas, particularly when combining wine with food. Soon you will be comparing various styles of wine and developing food and wine preferences. Begin reading articles in magazines and newspapers to fine tune your tastes. Lastly, gather with people who share your enthusiasm for food and wine, participate in group tastings and seminars. The best teacher of wine is experience, continue to experiment and you will learn. You do not have to become a scholar of wine to enjoy its pleasures and benefits when consumed responsibly.

Q: I have enjoyed wine for years, before it was "in vogue". I'm curious as to why you may think the subject of wine has so much appeal?

A: Wine has a certain mystique that entices the curiosity and desire in the general public. Wine, given the right combination of grapes, weather, aging and winemaker ability, is often as complex a commodity as an alluring painting, a compelling novel or a synchronized symphony. It is more than just another food or beverage. Wine is as much an art form as it is a scientific phenomena and an agricultural product. The more one learns about this alluring subject, the more enjoyment and appreciation is derived from its experiences. Wine is versatile and all giving, from an unassuming companion with a meal to a position of cultural significance and social status. As with many other art forms, man has created a love affair with wine as an extension of his desire to intermingle and become one with all that is natural and reaches the soul.

Q: I've been told that the most important element in tasting wine is in the sense of smell and not taste. Why is this so?

A: The greatest proportion of what we normally consider to be taste or flavor is actually smell. When wine is sniffed, the olfactory or odor-sensitive portion of the nose is opened and collects information that is transmitted to the brain. Additional information reaches the olfactory region when one tastes the wine and exhales through the nose. This aerates and warms the wine sufficiently to release more volatile components. The smell combined with the tongue's contribution of the taste sensations, sweet, sour, salty and bitter, all add to the full pleasure of the wine. As an experiment, hold your nose as you sip a little wine and notice how much flavor is missing compared to using both senses. The sensation is similar to trying to taste food with a cold.

Q: What is a "waiter's" corkscrew?

A: The "waiter's" corkscrew is the one that looks like a folded jackknife. Its spiral screw unfolds to a "T" with a leverage grip at one end and a cutting knife at the other. It's called a "waiter's" corkscrew because it is compact and easy for service people to carry around in their pocket. It does, however, take some practice to become proficient with its use. The simplest and most inexpensive corkscrew to have around the kitchen is the popular "wing" corkscrew. The handles of this opener go up as the screw is turned into the cork. When the auger is all the way in, the handles are pushed down, forcing the cork up and out. Do not use a corkscrew in opening a bottle of champagne, however. Use only your hands with the aid of a towel. Carefully twist the bottle with one hand while holding the cork with the other so the pressure inside will gradually force the cork out nice and easy.

Q: Is there any way to prevent a cork from breaking when opening a bottle of wine?

A: Most broken wine corks are due to inadequate corkscrews or poor technique in opening a bottle. First of all, you know you have the proper corkscrew when you can place a toothpick up the center of the "worm". This type of auger will give a better grip in the cork, particularly if the cork is fragile. Secondly, be sure you screw the "worm" down the middle far enough to pierce the bottom of the cork and then pull out steadily. Twisting, jerking and bending a corkscrew in a cork will only increase your chances of losing a firm hold and breaking the cork, or even worse, striping the core. With all your care, a cork may still break off in the bottle. At this point, try the corkscrew again or push the remaining solid cork into the bottle and carefully pour the wine over the cork and into a clear glass decanter to be used to serve the wine.

Q: I opened a bottle of white wine that had some crystals on the bottom of the cork and in the bottom of the bottle. What is it and is it harmless?

A: The crystals are the result of Tartaric acid, which is the principal acid in wine made from ripe grapes. They are not harmful and are natural deposits of the wine. This suspicious looking substance is also know as Cream of Tartar. It is a by-product of the wine used in the manufacture of baking powder. If you find an accumulation of Cream of Tartar crystals in a bottle of wine, you need only allow the material to settle to the bottom and carefully pour off the clear wine into a clean, fresh container. Now you can enjoy your wine with complete peace of mind.

Q: What elements should one look for in evaluating a quality wine?

A: First and foremost, the wine must be free of defects such as off odors and tastes, based on your first impression. The color should be clear and brilliant. If the wine is appealing to the eye, it signals our other senses of taste and smell to be prepared for a pleasing experience. The fragrance of wine is as important as flavor, since our nose, more than anything else, influences our sense of taste. To be a truly fine quality wine, flavors should be complex and produce different taste sensations with each smell or sip. Yet, they should be balanced. If the wine is sweet, it should be offset with acidity or it will taste flat. If it is dry, there should be no harshness and the wine must have body and substance. Otherwise, it will appear thin and watery. Young wines should have full fruit flavor and aroma while older wines entice with intriguing nuances from barrel or bottle aging. Above all else, a wine must be pleasing to your individual taste and nobody can dictate that to you.

Q: How do professionals judge wines in competition and award medals?

A: All competitions have different methods, but a good guideline is the one used by Tasters Guild International in their annual wine evaluation. To be fair and unbiased, the wines are always tasted "blind" (the labels of the wines are not exposed until after they have been evaluated). Only the variety of the grapes, vintage year, degree of sweetness, and price category are made known to the tasters to evaluate the quality of the wine, the skill of the winemaker, and the perceived consumer value of the product. The actual evaluation of the wines are based on a cumulative twenty-point system. First, using a clear, stemmed glass, the wine is examined as to the clarity of color. Is it cloudy or clear? Is the color correct for the type of wine being evaluated? Various grape varieties produce diverse color hues and tones (0-2 points awarded). Next, is the sense of smell. The grape variety used should be recognizable by the fragrance or aroma (0-2). The bouquet is slightly different from aroma and is the result of proper fermentation, handling and aging of the wine with its many complex factors intertwined (0-2 points). Sensitive taste buds will detect the wine's natural acid content. If there is too much acid, the wine will be very tart and sour, if there is too little, the wine will be flat and flabby (0-2 points). The wine's acid must balance with sugar content to achieve the desired clean, crisp taste of fruit essence (0-2 points). There should also be a desired complexity in the makeup of wine and yet, the taste should have a distinct flavor of the grape variety and balance with the fruit aroma (0-3 points). In the case of red wines, the wine should have a slight astringency, much like the puckering effect of lemon juice (0-1 point). This is the result of tannin which allows the wine to age properly. Up to two additional points is allowed for the body or feel of the wine within the mouth. There should be the obvious presence of substance or density on the palate as opposed to being thin and watery. Finally, personal judgment and experience makes the conclusive assessment as to the overall general quality of the wine by the pleasant lingering finish that says it is all in perfect harmony (0-4 points). When the scores are tallied, 18-20 earns a gold; 16-17.9 is awarded a silver and 14-15.9 receives the bronze.

Q: Would you please explain the meaning of "foxy," "cloying" and "oxidized" in reference to tasting wine?

A: "Foxy" is the term used to identify the pronounced "grapey" flavor in wines from native American grape varieties (e.g. Concord and Niagara) usually found in grape juice and jelly. "Cloying" describes a wine that has too much sweetness and too little acidity. "Oxidized" refers to a wine that has lost its freshness from too much contact with oxygen.

Q: I've always used the guideline of "white wine with white meat and red wine with red meat." Does this still apply?

A: It's still a pretty good rule of thumb, but today's cooking is much more sophisticated and complex. Many of the old cooking "laws" are being thrown out the window by enterprising young chefs who are constantly looking for new and different approaches to making food more interesting. Look around, many fish and chicken dishes are now served with red sauces and beef with cream and herb sauces. Now, what wine do you serve? The key is to try different combinations of food and wine. There really is no set rule and it is quite acceptable to have a light red wine with a spicy Cajun seafood dish or a hearty white wine with a beef entree. There are still flavor combinations of food that are more naturally complemented by certain wines, but the main objective in today's liberal society is to enjoy what you are eating and the wine you are drinking. Experiment and let your palate be your guide.

Q: In my collection of wines I have both half bottles and regular size bottles of the same wine and vintage. I have found that the taste of the wine differs between the two bottle sizes. I purchased the wine at the same time and store them next to each other. Does the size of the bottle have an effect on the wine?

A: Yes, indeed. In general, the bigger the bottle the better the wine will keep. Wine has a constantly changing natural life span and the effective length of life, speed of maturity and level of ultimate quality are all in direct proportion to bottle size. Half-bottles are designed primarily for the restaurant trade where it is a convenient portion size for dining patrons. I would suggest full (750ml) bottles or better yet, magnum (1.5L) bottles, for future purchases for your collection.

Q: I want to build a wine cellar in my basement and would like suggestions for racks, insulation, etc. Can you make any suggestions?

A: Wine cellars can be as elaborate as your checkbook allows or as simple as a storage closet. The important thing to remember is that wine should be stored in an area that is free of vibration, does not encounter direct sunlight and has a relatively constant cool temperature. If you anticipate a large investment in wine to be stored over a number of years then a professionally built cellar may be in order. Storage of rare vintage wines should be in a controlled temperature of around 55 F. Storage racks, of just about any material, should be designed to fit the available space and accommodate wine bottles that are laid on their sides to keep the corks moist. The ideal situation for the long-term storage of fine rare wines is an air-conditioned room built on the outside foundation of the home and insulated sufficiently to keep out the influences of the home's heat-producing units. For shorter time storage (under two years) a simple enclosed area where the temperature does not vary more than ten degrees from 60 F at any one time of the year will work well for a constantly changing inventory. For more detailed information consult professional builders of saunas and wine vaults or many wine reference books give instructions and layouts of wine storage areas.

Q: I've been told to use round clay tiles for storing and keeping my collection of wine cool. Is this the best way to store wine bottles?

A: The tiles work well if you have the room. Since they take up a lot of valuable storage space, I would suggest storing six to twelve wine bottles on top of each other in sections partitioned by wood. This is the most efficient use of space and it allows air circulation around the glass bottles which is the most important factor in keeping all the bottles cool.

Q: So much has been written on the overindulgence of alcohol, but isn't alcohol and particularly wine, healthful when consumed in moderation?

A: Doctors are one of the largest occupational groups that participate in wine and food societies and clubs. They also encourage the use of moderate wine consumption because of its rich source of nutrients and the role it plays as a natural tranquilizer. Science has known for years that wine contains rich deposits of vitamins, minerals and natural sugars that are often times beneficial to good health. Red wines have more of these elements due to the juice's longer contact with the grapes' skin which add to the mix. Red wines, are rich in B vitamins derived from the grape skins. Both red and white wines contain important amounts of iron and contain less calories than most people think. A bottle of red or white dry wine contains about 500 calories. This will vary according to the combination of sugar and alcohol. Wine is also rich in potassium, low in sodium and works toward lowering cholesterol levels. Wine has long been used to fortify weak blood and to help ease sleeping problems. According to Dr. Russell V. Lee, Clinical Professor of Medicine, Stanford University School of Medicine, "There is no doubt at all that the moderate use of wine while eating is the most effective tranquilizer known to medical man." The key, like anything else, is not to abuse a good thing with overindulgence. Enjoy wine responsibly and common sense will tell you not to drink and drive.

Also Available!

RECIPES
FROM THE WINERIES
OF THE GREAT LAKES

In his first book, WINERIES OF THE GREAT LAKES: *A Guidebook,* Joe Borrello clued us in on one of the great hidden secrets of the Great Lakes region; that it is home to dozens of wineries that are producing many world class wines. His guidebook showed readers how to travel the highways and byways of the Great Lakes and discover these hidden treasures. Since Joe believes that food and wine are a natural combination, his new book, RECIPES FROM THE WINERIES OF THE GREAT LAKES seems a natural outgrowth of his research. In this book Joe tells you how to use the wine from your favorite Great Lakes winery to prepare some delicious and sumptuous meals. Featuring everything from appetizers, to main courses, to desserts, over 150 recipes from dozens of participating wineries are included in RECIPES FROM THE WINERIES OF THE GREAT LAKES.

Each recipe offers a complete nutritional breakdown, featuring the number of calories, fat grams, and all other dietary information. Substitutions for ingredients are also provided. Each recipe has been tested and reviewed by a variety of culinary professionals.

The book also includes a unique and interesting appendix featuring fun and interesting tips about tasting and cooking with wine.

ORDER INFORMATION

$17.00 each plus $3.50 shipping and handling

CREDIT CARDS ACCEPTED
Send check, money order, or credit card number and expiration date to:

Spradlin & Associates
PO Box 863
Lapeer, MI   48446

PHONE OR FAX ORDERS
Phone (810) 664-8406
Fax (810) 667-6719
Fax orders must include credit card information.